Contents

MANAGEMENT & CONSULTING:

An Introduction to James O. McKinsey

William B. Wolf

ILR Paperback Number 17
New York State School of
Industrial and Labor Relations
Cornell University

Library of Congress Catalog Card Number: 78-11840
International Standard Book Number: 0-87546-071-2

Copies of this book can be ordered from
ILR Publications Division
New York State School of Industrial and Labor Relations
Cornell University, Box 1000
Ithaca, New York 14853

Library of Congress Cataloging in Publication Data
Wolf, William B
    Management & consulting.
    (ILR paperback; no. 17)
    "Principal writings of James O. McKinsey": p.
    Includes index.
    1. Business consultants — United States. 2. McKinsey,
James Oscar 1889 – 1937. I. Title.   II. Series.
HD69.C6W64   658.4'0092'4   78-11840
ISBN 0-87546-071-2

Preface

This book is written for administrators, consultants, and students of management. It is, in effect, a guide to those who manage or wish to manage. Moreover, it is a book on how to consult. It grew out of my interest in developing a practical means for dealing with the problems of formal organizations. Over the years, as I have studied the work of major contributors to management, it has become evident that a book on James Oscar McKinsey could be helpful. His contribution is significant. Yet, in many respects, it is lost to the current literature on management.

McKinsey contributed both to the theory and practice of management. He was a pioneer in developing budgetary control, managerial accounting, business policy, and a managerial approach to finance. He established the consulting firm McKinsey and Company, which is today one of the largest and best known in the world. He was chairman of the board of Marshall Field and Company, one of the world's largest retailing firms. What makes McKinsey's contribution most impressive is that he accomplished so much in a short life-span: he died at the age of forty-eight.

A review of the current literature shows scarcely a reference to McKinsey. Moreover, among my colleagues he is only associated with the consulting firm that bears his name. Because of this and because I have found his ideas extremely provocative, I have written this book, hoping thereby to provide a synthesis of McKinsey's approach to consulting. Here is a practitioner's approach. It is one of the few that is available and hence should be a contribution to the consulting profession.

In a sense I feel some inadequacies in this undertaking. My qualifications come from working in McKinsey's shadow rather than from firsthand knowledge of the man. I have attempted to locate his unpublished papers but the search has not been very rewarding — only some consulting reports and a speech.

Most of the material for this book comes from a careful

reading of McKinsey's published works and from the help of his former associates. Both Professor Lewis Sorrel and Professor Samuel Nerlove, formerly of the Graduate School of Business of the University of Chicago, were important in this effort. It was in conversations with them that I first became aware of McKinsey's contributions to management.

The cooperation of others close to McKinsey has been much beyond what an author expects or hopes for. Billy Goetz, Marvin Bower, John G. Neukom, and William H. Newman carefully read and critiqued early drafts of this manuscript. They corrected facts, supplied original material, and made editorial comments. The significance of their contributions is indicated by the fact that all of them worked closely with McKinsey.

Others who aided in this endeavor include Walter McKinsey, a nephew of James O. McKinsey; Robert McKinsey, one of McKinsey's sons; and Michael McManus of Ithaca College. Professor McManus's interest in "the professor-consultant" caused him to dig and probe into McKinsey's work and to interview Marvin Bower. In addition, Professor McManus did some of the library research for this project.

Probably my main qualification for writing this book comes from the fact that I shared with McKinsey the Zeitgeist of the Graduate School of Business of the University of Chicago. True, he died ten years before I arrived there, but in my six years at the University of Chicago, I absorbed much of the same outlook. In fact, my philosophy of management, which I had always thought developed from my own experience and study, is closely akin to McKinsey's.

Another factor that prepared me to write this book arose from an assignment I had as a consultant to McKinsey and Company. My assignment was to study a special management system that the firm had developed. In retrospect it was an adaptation of McKinsey's ideas on budgeting, updated by computer technology.

Finally, I am deeply indebted for assistance and support to my colleagues and the staff at the New York State School of Industrial and Labor Relations. I am especially appreciative of the assistance given by Jo Churey, Lynn Johnson, and Terry Schuster.

WILLIAM B. WOLF   *NYSSILR, Cornell University*
                                   May 1978

Chronology
James Oscar McKinsey

1889	Born in Gamma, Missouri, June 4.
1912	Received the Pd.B. degree from State Teacher's College, Warrensburg, Missouri.
1913	Received the LL.B. degree from University of Arkansas, Fayetteville, Arkansas.
1914	Taught bookkeeping in St. Louis and took courses at St. Louis University.
1915	Received a scholarship to the School of Commerce, University of Chicago.
1916	Received the Ph.B. degree from University of Chicago.
1917	Appointed to the faculty of the University of Chicago. Joined the U.S. Army as a private.
1918	Promoted to Lieutenant in the U.S. Army, Ordnance Department.
1919	Passed the State of Illinois C.P.A. examination. Received the M.A. degree from University of Chicago.
1920	Joined the firm of Frazer and Torbet (1920–25). Lectured in accounting at Columbia University.
1921	Appointed Assistant Professor of Accounting at University of Chicago.
1923	Became Vice President of the American Association of University Instructors in Accounting.
1924	Became President of the American Association of University Instructors in Accounting.

1925	Became senior partner, James O. McKinsey & Co. (1925 – 35).
1926	Appointed Professor of Business Policy, University of Chicago (1926 – 35).
1935	Elected Chairman of the Board, Marshall Field & Co. (1935 – 37).
1936	Elected Chairman of the Board, American Management Association.
1937	Died in Chicago, Illinois, November 30.

Chapter I

A Brief Biography of James O. McKinsey

This book deals with the art of management and the skill of managerial consulting. It focuses on the life and work of James Oscar McKinsey. There are two basic reasons for this.

First, McKinsey was a successful teacher, consultant, and top-level executive. Not only was he successful, but he pioneered many of the concepts which today stand at the forefront of management theory. Hence, a reexamination of his ideas should help in developing insights into effective management.

The second reason for dealing with McKinsey is that most of us find it easier to grasp ideas if we can relate them to specific personalities. We can usually comprehend the subtleties of a man's approach to management much better if we can put that person into perspective by learning something of his life and career.

Activities and Accomplishments McKinsey began as a barefoot hillbilly in the Ozarks. He was born and raised in a three-room farmhouse near Mexico, Missouri. His father was a farmer, and throughout his early life McKinsey knew poverty. While McKinsey was in high school, the principal, who was also superintendent of the district, hired McKinsey to teach high school algebra in a special training program for teachers. This was to be a pattern in his future career. As William Newman, one of McKinsey's protégés recalled: "When Mac was in a mellow mood and got talking about himself, he used to claim that wherever he went to school, he ended up teaching in that school before he obtained his degree."[1]

After completing high school, McKinsey went to the

State Teacher's College at Warrensburg, Missouri. There he earned a degree of Bachelor of Pedagogy. In 1913, McKinsey received a Bachelor of Laws degree from the University of Arkansas in Fayetteville. He never took a great interest in law, and in later years he seldom mentioned his legal training. One of his colleagues explained this by observing: "Well in those days [1913] Mac probably took a few courses and read some books on law and decided he'd take the examinations. With his brilliant mind, he had no difficulty passing."[2] From Fayetteville, McKinsey went to St. Louis, Missouri. There he studied and taught bookkeeping. At this time he met James W. Baker, president of the South-Western Publishing Company, who later became McKinsey's principal publisher.

From St. Louis, McKinsey went to the University of Chicago, where, in 1916, he received his Bachelor of Philosophy degree and started a master's program. His education was interrupted by World War I. He entered the army as a private and soon advanced to the rank of lieutenant in the Ordnance Department. This wartime experience had a significant influence on his subsequent career. As he recalled, he used to deal with important suppliers for the army. This caused him to travel all over the United States, and he is alleged to have remarked that the experience "opened his eyes to the need for skilled consultants to help management improve its effectiveness."[3]

After World War I, McKinsey returned to the University of Chicago, completed his master's degree, and became a certified public accountant in the state of Illinois. While at the university, McKinsey caught the attention of George Frazer, who was professor of accounting. In 1917, before McKinsey had earned his degree, Frazer hired him as an instructor in accounting. In 1920, Frazer hired McKinsey to work in his firm of public accountants, Frazer and Torbet. He sent McKinsey to New York City to help establish an office of the firm; while there, McKinsey lectured in accounting at Columbia University.

McKinsey returned to Chicago in 1921. Still a member of the firm of Frazer and Torbet, he became assistant professor of accounting at the University of Chicago.

Starting around 1919, McKinsey began writing at a feverish pace. One of his first publications was a monograph entitled *Federal Income and Excess Profits Tax Laws*.[4] This was a teacher's guide to the revenue act of 1918. It was given first as a series of lectures in 1919 for the Chicago

Chapter of the American Institute of Banking. In 1920, it was completely revised and published by South-Western Publishing Company.

In 1920, McKinsey collaborated with A. C. Hodges to write *Principles of Accounting*, published by the University of Chicago Press.[5] This text was part of the grand scheme developed by Leon C. Marshall, then dean of the School of Commerce. Marshall provided the central thrust for the developing philosophy of the school of business at the University of Chicago. In the process, he encouraged the younger men on the faculty to write books in selected areas; *Principles of Accounting* was one of these books.

In 1920, McKinsey also published the first volume of *Bookkeeping and Accounting*, and the following year he completed volume two.[6] These two volumes were written for students in secondary schools. In many ways they were the precursor of McKinsey's classic book *Budgetary Control*.[7]

McKinsey's theme in his bookkeeping and accounting books is consistent and uniform. First, he did not like the term "bookkeeping." He preferred to include it under "accounting." This terminology allowed him to adhere to a more comprehensive view of bookkeeping, one which emphasized its use to those who managed. In this way McKinsey blended bookkeeping into what today would be considered basic accounting. Second, McKinsey maintained that in our society educated people should understand the method of collecting and presenting statistical and accounting data so that these materials can be used by management. His emphasis was on general principles and their applications to the solution of business problems. This approach stood in marked contrast to the usual high school bookkeeping course of his day, which emphasized routines and techniques. McKinsey summarized his point of view in the preface to the 1926 edition of *Bookkeeping and Accounting*: "This text is based on the assumption that the function of bookkeeping records is to provide information which can be *used in the management of a business*."[8] In *Bookkeeping and Accounting* McKinsey continually called on the student to analyze transactions and to consider how their effects would be shown in accounting reports. "The student is taught to look at the records from the point of view of the manager rather than from the point of view of the bookkeeper."[9]

In these books McKinsey emphasized that accounting should teach the student to reason analytically. He felt that as an approach for developing analytical ability accounting was on a par with any other course in the university.

In 1922, while McKinsey was still a consultant in the firm of Frazer and Torbet, and assistant professor of accounting in the School of Commerce and Administration of the University of Chicago, he published three books. One of these books was the *Organization and Methods of the Walworth Manufacturing Company.* [10] It is a detailed description of the Walworth Company — its history, organization, methods, and changes that it experienced. It is the kind of case study that helps students develop insight into the functioning of an organization as a whole, and which also familiarizes them with the detailed problems of policy, decision making, and control. The philosophy underlying the case is that students need to see the firm holistically; that is, they need to envision all of the parts and their interaction so that they can deal intelligently with the problems of the firm.

In 1922, McKinsey also published a two-volume work called *Financial Management.* [11] It was part of a series edited by George Frazer and the authors were picked by Frazer himself. [12]

Financial Management continued the McKinsey approach by studying the problems of financial management as they arise in the normal operations of a going concern. Taking the point of view of the treasurer or chief financial executive of the business, McKinsey emphasized the internal problems of financial management — determining and budgeting capital requirements, securing capital and controlling capital and its use — as contrasted with the problems that arise from the external relations of a business. The book thus represented a shift from the theme then prevailing in financial texts, which promoted reorganizations, consolidations, mergers, receiverships, and the like. In other words, McKinsey focused on everyday experiences in the management of finance. As could be expected, he stressed budgeting, accounting, and statistical methods of control, and in that sense, the book represented an application of scientific management to financial planning and control. McKinsey made it clear, however, that he was stating the problems rather than offering full solutions to them. His goal was to stimulate thought as well as to improve understanding.

Budgetary Control was probably the outstanding book published by McKinsey. This book has been recognized by many authorities as a classic. Carl Heyel, writing in the

Encyclopedia of Management, stated that McKinsey "focused attention on the importance of budgeting as a major instrument of management, and wrote the first standard book on the subject."[13] L. P. Alford, the noted management authority, also recognized the importance of McKinsey's work in the area of budgetary control. In 1933 he wrote: "Budgets made extraordinary progress following the publication in 1922 of *Budgetary Control* by J. O. McKinsey. No other mechanism of management of similar scope and complexity has ever been introduced so rapidly. . . . It is estimated that 80 percent of the budgets installed in industry have been put in since 1922."[14]

Probably most indicative of the dramatic effect of McKinsey's book on budgeting are the comments of Harry A. Hopf, an outstanding American management authority. In 1945, Hopf was asked to prepare a list of works he regarded as indispensable in the field of management. Among the twelve titles chosen by Hopf was McKinsey's book *Budgetary Control.* The following is Hopf's comment:

Although this work was written in 1922, and a great deal has been written on the subject of budgeting in the past twenty years, Professor McKinsey's text has lost none of its value with the passage of time; it must still be regarded as an outstanding contribution. The author, whose untimely death in 1937 terminated a brilliant career as teacher, professional consultant and business executive, was noted for the penetrating character of his thinking and the lasting quality of his contributions to the solution of business problems. He was particularly gifted in the art of exposition, a fact of which there is abundant evidence in his writings.[15]

What makes *Budgetary Control* such a significant contribution is its clarity and its point of view. It presents the process of budgetary control as an integrating device for gaining a broad understanding of the problems of administration. Moreover, the book draws heavily upon McKinsey's practical experience in consulting. It provides illustrations and examples and continually emphasizes a comprehensive understanding of the entire organization. The presentation helps the readers make the necessary adjustments and accommodations to fit the specific needs of their own organizations. What stands out if one reads *Budgetary Control* today is that it is, in effect, a book on what is currently fashionable as "Management by Objectives." McKinsey's advice and techniques for establishing and managing budgets are as relevant today as ever. Furthermore, with the advent of on-line computer processing of data, his ideas take on new relevance.

In 1923, McKinsey collaborated with Stuart P. Meech to write *Controlling the Finances of a Business*.[16] In commenting about this book, Professor William Newman stated:

The book with Stuart Meech on Controlling the Finances of a Business *never cut much ice. But the book was distinctive because it took the viewpoint of the treasurer and what somebody running company finances ought to be thinking. At that time, and until quite recently, most of the financial texts had a strong institutional orientation and told about the different kinds of financial instruments. McKinsey understood all of this but said, "Now looking at it from the point of view of the financial management of the company what are the problems?" Consequently, he worked on cash flow and the sources of capital and how one manages sources of capital. If you go back to the early days I guess Gerstenberg had a chapter or two on this. But it is only recently that books in finance have adopted a managerial orientation. McKinsey took financial information and gave it a basic managerial orientation.*[17]

In 1924 McKinsey published two landmark texts: *Business Administration*,[18] and *Managerial Accounting*.[19] The latter was planned as a two-volume opus, but McKinsey never published the second volume.

Business Administration was among the early texts on policy. Its goal was to provide students with an understanding of the organization and management of business firms. Its emphasis was on why managers do things rather than how they do them. In the design of the book, McKinsey used a "functional-process" approach. Namely, he dealt with the functional areas of organizations such as marketing, production, personnel, finance, and standards and records. He examined how these functions are managed, pointing out continually that the management process will be carried out differently in different organizational settings. This is currently labeled by management theorists as "a contingency approach to management." The last chapter of the book is a detailed case which interrelates and brings together the functional areas. Thus, it provides a holistic approach to business problems. The last question in the book — where McKinsey asked his students to "illustrate concretely how this case shows the existence and interdependence of the personnel, marketing, finance, and standards and records functions of business administration" — captures the tone of the text.[20]

Managerial Accounting was a pioneering book. In its preface, McKinsey stated that the book grew out of five years of experiments conducted at the University of Chicago, but anybody who reads McKinsey's works chronologically starting with the bookkeeping text will see this book as part of a natural continuum in McKinsey's writing. The primary goal of *Managerial Accounting* is to teach students how accounting data can be used to solve business problems. Here again, McKinsey emphasized the need for students to develop analytical thinking. The questions which he put at the ends of chapters forced the students to think analytically: "With few exceptions the questions cannot be answered by memorizing text material. They constantly require the thinking through of new problems and the application of the information obtained from the text material to new situations."[21]

In this book, McKinsey continued to use a functional-process approach to management. He analyzed his subjects in terms of the functional areas of management and saw the process of management, the task of the executive, as one of organizing, preparing and directing the "agencies of production to make a product of value to the human race and a profit to the producers."[22] In carrying out these tasks, McKinsey considered records the basis of management — essential in organizing, directing, and controlling operations.

In 1924, McKinsey collaborated with James L. Palmer in writing a section on budgeting for L. P. Alford's *Management's Handbook*.[23] In doing so, McKinsey and Palmer began a relationship that carried on into later years. At the time, Palmer was an instructor in accounting at the University of Chicago, School of Commerce and Administration. Later, McKinsey brought him into Marshall Field and Company where he eventually became president. The section in *Management's Handbook* is a forty-six-page condensation of much of McKinsey's earlier book on budgeting.

Management's Handbook reflects the spirit of the times in which McKinsey was developing his ideas and coming to the fore in the field of management. The *Handbook* itself is an attempt to do for management what had been done for engineering — to assemble a practical compendium of techniques and ideas to guide managers in their tasks. In a sense, it is more an industrial engineering handbook than a management handbook, in that it emphasizes quantitative techniques, scientific method, and the like. In this respect, it is a reflection of the period between 1918 and 1929 during which the American economy was recovering from World War I and moving into "the roaring twenties." A revolution by mass production and manufacturing was going on. The boom was taking off. During this time the early scientific management movement blossomed and reached its zenith. This is reflected in *Management's Handbook*. For example, the first section in the *Handbook* deals with mathematical tables and statistics, the next section deals with mathematics, and many of the 1,607 pages are taken up with practical discussions of subjects such as charts, forms, classification and symbols, quality control, procurement, and motion and time study.

It is important to see McKinsey in this context. Frequently, a man expresses the spirit of his time, and for McKinsey this seems to be the case. He started out in bookkeeping and accounting and then developed the field of budgeting. Next, he moved to the field of managerial accounting. In short, he emphasized quantitative methods of management. In part his focus resulted from the fact that around 1918 corporations were beginning to develop data to satisfy the federal income tax law. McKinsey believed that this information should be used for managerial purposes.

In his managerial approach and in much of his philosophy, McKinsey also reflected his training at the University of Chicago. He came to the University around 1914. There he received the degree of Bachelor of Philosophy and began work on his master's degree. The School of Commerce and Administration at the University of Chicago was at this time in its formative years. It had been founded in 1898, but had not really gained momentum until 1909 when Leon C. Marshall became dean.

It was Marshall who shaped the school. Under him the general philosophy of the school was formed and publicized. He reorganized the curriculum, attracted an outstanding faculty, and emphasized the relationship of business to society. His point of view was that "the study of business administration falls little short of being as broad and inclusive as life itself."[24] Marshall was interested in a managerial approach to almost all of the sciences to show their relationships to the administration of business. John Neukom, who attended the University of Chicago in the 1930s and later was manager of the San Francisco office of McKinsey and Company, observed:

We had at the University of Chicago in those days a very interesting faculty. One of the strongest faculties I've seen. These guys went out and practiced what they preached. Later they were all howling successes. My advertising professor was James Webb Young. He became head of J. Walter Thompson. Then there was Jim Palmer, Ted Yntema, L. C. Sorrell,

In 1925, McKinsey left the firm of Frazer and Torbet to establish his own firm, James O. McKinsey and Company. This was the start of the firm that still bears his name and prospers. The split between McKinsey and Frazer was inevitable. Billy Goetz, who knew both men, recalls them each as having "to be head of whatever he was in, and even, perhaps, a little more than that. He had to be acknowledged as head by everyone else in the organization."[26]

McKinsey continued to teach at the University of Chicago, and in 1926 he became professor of business policy. It is significant to note that he had dropped the emphasis on accounting and was much more involved with the overall management of organizations. He was among the first professors of business policy in the United States. His work in this field was highly innovative and pioneering; he emphasized the need of the student to see the whole enterprise, and the interrelationship of the whole and the parts. In later years, business policy became the capstone course in schools of business administration. The accrediting association, the American Assembly of Collegiate Schools of Business, eventually required a business school to offer a policy course before it would grant it accreditation.

From 1925 to 1935 McKinsey concentrated his efforts on consulting. At the University of Chicago he was recognized as an outstanding professor, but he was not too deeply involved in university affairs. In reflecting on this period Professor Newman observed: "McKinsey took off on his own. He became absorbed in consulting and in applying ideas. While he maintained his affiliation with the school until the time he became chairman of the board of Marshall Field, he only gave his courses and took no significant part in other faculty activities."[27]

After 1927, McKinsey taught only business policy and was no longer involved in managerial accounting. Nor was he involved in research or Ph.D. Committees. He simply taught an early morning class and then rushed to his office to participate in his consulting practice. John Neukom recalled:

He always had classes at 8:00 in the morning. He thought that it was a good use of his time to get the class over before 9:00 so that he could get down to the office to conduct his professional practice for the rest of the day. He lived in the neighborhood, in the Cloisters. It was easy to walk over to class at 8:00 in the morning. His car picked him up after class and took him to the office.[28]

As a consultant, McKinsey became interested in winning friends and securing clients. Therefore he was extremely active in outside activities. In particular he played an important role in the American Management Association: he was one of its founders and its second president, he served as chairman of its board of directors, and he wrote numerous articles for its publications.

In 1929, McKinsey published *Accounting Principles,* which is still one of the best-selling books in the field.[29] The book is a refinement and revision of the original *Bookkeeping and Accounting.* In 1935 *Accounting Principles* was revised by H. J. Nobel; still later, after McKinsey's death, the book appeared under the authorship of Noble and Niswanger; and in 1976, the book continued under the authorship of Niswanger and Fess. Total sales of all editions may have exceeded those of any other accounting book. The book is important as a pioneer in presenting accounting as a field that every educated person in modern society should understand. McKinsey thought that the first course in accounting should contribute to the liberal education of the students rather than preparing them to become specialists in the field. This philosophy now prevails in accounting textbooks.

McKinsey's consulting practice grew rapidly. He hired a number of men and gained a reputation in both New York and Chicago as one of the best consultants in the business. In 1935, after directing a comprehensive study of Marshall Field and Company, he was offered the chairmanship of its board. He weighed the decision carefully. His son Robert recalled that his father paced the living room and talked it out with his mother. In essence, Robert remembered that what attracted McKinsey to the job at Marshall Field was the challenge. He felt he had been rather glibly telling people what to do and now he wanted to prove that he could do it himself. It was to be his test to bring theory and practice together. Once this was done he planned to return to McKinsey and Company.

At that time, Marshall Field was still feeling the effects of the Depression. It became McKinsey's job to get rid of dead wood and unprofitable divisions. He had to cut whole divisions, retire people early, fire old-timers, and take other drastic steps. Robert McKinsey recalled that in the process of managing Marshall Field, his father received between ten and twenty letters threatening his life. His son Richard recalled that the job put pressure on his father and at one time he was so depressed by it that he considered resigning and going back to consulting sooner than planned.

In the end McKinsey did save Marshall Field but he did it at tremendous cost. He undermined his health, and on returning from one of his trips to Fieldcrest Mills in North Carolina, he contracted pneumonia. This was in 1937 before the discovery of the sulfa drugs and penicillin. Within a short period McKinsey had succumbed. He died November 30, 1937.

McKinsey's success at Marshall Field was widely recognized. At the time of his death a tribute to him appeared in *American Business*.

A MANAGEMENT ENGINEER

There comes a time in the life of every business when it needs a good shaking up. As the business gathers years it also gathers barnacles — old employees who have lost their drive and have settled down to a complacent middle age. James O. McKinsey, a college professor, writer of books on accounting, and a management engineer of distinction, was engaged in 1935 by the directors of Marshall Field and Company to pull them out of the red. There was no alternative open to the Field directors. The business had lost $12,000,000 in the five previous operating years. It was a tough assignment and one that called for a ruthless disregard of sentiment and a cold-blooded facing of facts. So every activity of the great business was analyzed to determine whether or not it was self-supporting. One department after another was liquidated. Wholesaling activities of the business were suspended. Hundreds of employees who had outlived their usefulness were pensioned or dropped. Office and administration methods were systemized. Waste was patiently searched out and stopped. Financing was simplified. Under that type of management the red ink was changed to black. The operating statement for the first nine months of 1937 showed a profit of more than a million dollars, with the Christmas season still ahead! And then, as he stood upon the threshold of great achievement, death took James O. McKinsey, as it must one day take us all. He was only 48 years old. He died, as so many business men have died, a sacrifice to a job that made impossible demands upon his nervous energy. His untimely death not only deprives Marshall Field and Company of a directing genius, but deprives scientific management of its greatest practitioner. James O. McKinsey's career stands as a monument to the opportunity in modern business for the management engineer. His record with Marshall Field and Company proves, if proof be needed, that the difference between a profit and a loss, is nearly always a matter of management. [30]

McKinsey died in 1937 but his ideas and concepts were popularized by William H. Newman in *Business Policies and Management*, one of the most widely circulated books on business policy.[31] It is now in its seventh edition.[32] According to Newman:

This book actually originated in Marshall Field and Company. McKinsey became chairman of the board after the consulting firm had made a series of studies of the company. McKinsey had a real interest in training and getting people to do what he called "think right" or "think straight," so he organized a class that met between 8:00 and 9:00 A.M. once a week at the retail store. And oddly enough all the people who were invited to attend managed to get there at 8:00 and McKinsey gave them "the word." He was chairman of the board at the time and I was over there as his leg man — assistant to the chairman. He asked me to put together outlines based on the General Survey Outline—*the way of analysis that had been used by the consulting firm—so there I was producing outlines that we passed out to the executives.*

McKinsey never missed a chance to turn a buck if it wasn't too much trouble and he had written innumerable books. So he conceived of these morning meetings as a project which would not only be useful in training executives of the retail store but also would provide the basis of a book. This was the arrangement he had worked out with me, and since he had published with South-Western Publishing Company he talked to Ernest Crabbe who was their editor at that time. Both of them agreed that there would be a useful market for a general statement of what it took to run a business.

McKinsey died and Ernest Crabbe came to me: "Look I still think there is a market for this book." Then he proceeded to suggest some changes. McKinsey was interested in getting a skeleton or framework; Crabbe said while that may be useful, it would be much more saleable if we put in a whole series of illustrations of what McKinsey was actually talking about. So he encouraged me to fill in with examples.

Looking at the book then, and to some extent now, you will find that there is a pretty sharp, clear outline of issues and of possible ways to get at those issues. But interlarded with all this are examples that try to make the issues come to life.[33]

The first edition of *Business Policies and Management* adheres closely to McKinsey's framework for organizational diagnosis, and contains his photograph as well as many of the illustrations he used. Thus, many students have been taught McKinsey's framework.

The early editions of this text were dedicated to McKinsey and in the preface Newman acknowledged his intellectual debt. The seventh edition, however, is dedicated to Samuel Bronfman. The only reference to McKinsey in the 734 pages of this edition is the statement in the preface that: "the model [used in this book] is a lineal descendant of a diagnostic approach to company-wide problems used by James O. McKinsey, founder of the pre-eminent consulting 'firm'."[34] Thus, today, McKinsey is only casually associated with two of the significant books he inspired — *The Principles of Accounting,* which currently appears under the authorship of Niswanger and Fess, and *Strategy, Policy and Central Management,* which currently appears under the authorship of Newman and Logan.

A Picture of the Man

What kind of a man was McKinsey? How did he happen to make significant and pioneering developments in the field of management? The answer to these questions is, in part, that he was a man of his times, but it is more than that. Interviews with his colleagues revealed that he was a man who showed the imprint of his early childhood in the Ozarks. He had a strong need for status, considerable humility, and a compelling drive to achieve. One of his sons described him as a workaholic: he was at the office all day Saturday and brought work home on Sunday. What is more, the children were not allowed to make noise around the house when "Daddy" was working. He was not home very much and when he was, his son Robert recalled, McKinsey would talk out problems with his wife, but she was there more as a sounding board than to criticize constructively or suggest solutions to problems.

He was generally taciturn around the house. He seldom would bend or relax, though when he did he had a fine sense of humor. Most of the time, however, he was interested mainly in his work. His wife supported him in this. She respected and admired him tremendously and frequently would give dinner parties that were related to his consulting practice. At these dinner parties, the children were permitted to participate. In this way, they were exposed early to business activities.

McKinsey's sons felt the scars of his childhood. When they asked their father for bikes and toys he would tell them they were lucky to grow up with servants in the house and have all the other luxuries of their home. He was reluctant to spend on toys or other items he classed as nonessential.

As a poor farm boy McKinsey developed an interest in earning money and accumulating wealth. To a large measure money symbolized achievement and success for him. Whenever his economic circumstances improved he would move his family to a higher-class neighborhood. At one time they rented a large farm in Wheaton, Illinois, and at another a home in Lake Forest, Illinois. The first had been owned by the Ball family, the inventors of tops for Mason jars. It had a stable and a completely enclosed polo field. The house in Lake Forest was also a mansion with stables and riding facilities. As the economic good fortune of the McKinseys progressed, they moved to the North Side of Chicago. When McKinsey died, he had a country house as well as an apartment in one of Chicago's most prestigious neighborhoods, the 1500 block of Lake Shore Drive.

McKinsey not only needed achievement, but wanted tangible evidence of that achievement. His decision to become the chief executive officer at Marshall Field was part of this need.

Another characteristic that helps in understanding McKinsey was his phenomenal memory. Again and again, friends and colleagues recalled how he could observe minutiae, synthesize them, and come up with significant conclusions. His memory is reflected in his humor — he collected stories, which he used to illustrate points. John Neukom recalled one about a little old lady who went to the London zoo. She was attracted to the hippopotamus. She called to the keeper and asked, "Are you in charge of this animal?" He said yes. She asked, "What does the animal eat?" He told her. "How old is the animal?" He told her. She asked a series of informational questions. Finally she asked, "What is the animal's sex?" The keeper said, "I don't know." She said, "You're in charge of the animal and you don't know the sex of the animal? I think that's rank incompetence, you're not doing your job." He replied, "Madam, I always thought that was only of interest to another hippopotamus." McKinsey's point was that a lot of subjects discussed in the office were of interest only to other consulting firms, not to clients. McKinsey also used his stories to establish rapport, for camaraderie, and to relieve tensions. Neukom recalled one time when a group of consultants were on the road conducting a study. "It was late in the evening and Mac said he would match every man in the room story for story. And he did! Each man told his story and then Mac topped it."[35]

Although McKinsey pioneered in management, he never developed a school of thinking. His students did not band together to preserve his heritage; in fact, within twenty years of his death, his name was practically forgotten by scholars and practitioners. This was in spite of his many accomplishments, and raises the question why his name is associated only with the consulting firm he founded. To explore this question I interviewed several people. The findings are consistent. "McKinsey was more interested in being respected than loved." He had an affable manner, he was respected, he had charisma, and he made sense, but he did not have a personality that develops a closely knit group of disciples. Part of this was due to his own attitude. Newman summed this up succinctly when he observed: "McKinsey wasn't sentimental. There wasn't any kind of tenderness about him. Lo and behold if I ceased to be useful to him I think he would just say 'There's no go anymore'."[36] A reason contributing to McKinsey's failure to develop a school of thought was his preference for seeking new challenges. According to Newman:

McKinsey was not interested in theory as such and found practical problems quite intriguing. On the other hand, once he had thought through a problem and arrived at what seemed to him to be a logical ~onclusion, he lost interest in that problem. Implementation of policy ᵢ.:cisions bored him. Also going over and over the same kind of problem ! ᵤred him. These mental characteristics affected both his conceptual work and the activities of the consulting firm. He had no interest in building up a consulting practice which installed budgetary procedures in company after company nor did he want to build a large consulting staff to do the kind of detailed work that Ford, Bacon & Davis found so profitable. His was an inquiring, restless mind. I think this had two important consequences. One was that he kept moving on to new problems and consequently made a whole series of contributions instead of sticking to just one. The second result is that by failing to persistently follow through, refine, and promote an idea his name did not become associated with that idea.[37]

Other comments help round out the picture of McKinsey. For example, in explaining the split between McKinsey and Frazer when McKinsey was a partner of Frazer and Torbet, Newman observed: "Each man was kind of an individual to himself and you just couldn't hold the two personalities in the same firm. McKinsey wanted to really call the shots. He thoroughly appreciated help and assistance but nevertheless wanted work done the way he was doing it. So his partners came and went, with the exception of Tom Kearney."[38] Billy Goetz gives a feeling for McKinsey's priorities in this vignette:

On one occasion McKinsey went to the office on Christmas Day to dictate a report. One of the secretaries had to go down to the office to take the dictation. In order to make up for her missing Christmas Day with her family, he gave her two days off later in the week. She didn't feel that that was quite fair for she would rather have had Christmas Day. But, that was partly to impress on his staff how serious business really was. The client came first![39]

McKinsey had a commanding and convincing way about him. John Neukom observed:

He was impressive, well tailored, and when he walked in a room everybody looked up. There was an immediate magnetism and attractiveness. He just had that drive and magnetism that attracted people. He was immediately the center of the meeting that he walked into. If he wasn't the center before, it was obvious the focal point would move over to him.

When asked if he could give the reasons for this, Neukom replied that he thought the major reason "was that most of the people who had experience with McKinsey realized that he had something worth saying and he ought to be listened to."[40]

Another aspect of McKinsey was his interest in training young men. As Newman explained, "Mac was always a teacher. He started out teaching in high school. He had his bachelor's degree in pedagogy and he started teaching at the University of Chicago before he completed his master's degree."[41] It was his interest in teaching that contributed so much to McKinsey's consulting firm.

Yet, on another level some people regarded McKinsey as tough and hard-boiled. McKinsey commented on this in a letter he sent to a partner in his consulting firm:

Although I am sure that you and many others who know me will never believe it, I am, in fact, a meek and simple soul who would rather indulge in philosophical thinking than be engaged in heated controversy. Notwithstanding this natural tendency, I have spent a considerable amount of my time during the last fifteen years in saying and doing things which should have been said and done by others, but which they hesitated to say and do. I assume this is due to the fact that because of my philosophical inclinations I have developed some tendency to think in a logical manner and when this thinking clearly indicates a conclusion I find it difficult to resist the temptation of stating it. Furthermore, when such a conclusion indicates definitely the need for action I feel I am rendering a service by trying to secure such action. I suppose I am doomed, therefore, to go through life doing things which make people think I am aggressive and hardboiled.[42]

McKinsey went on to say what he really thought about his partner's actions and why he should try to mend his ways.

Another important aspect of McKinsey's personality was his pleasure in associating with different people. He had special skills in working with individuals and small groups. With individuals, his pattern was to establish rapport and then to start asking questions rather than giving answers. In this manner he would diagnose the essence of the person's problem. After gathering sufficient data, he frequently had constructive ideas or suggestions to make.

Throughout, McKinsey had a narrow focus. He did not read very widely; he had no interest in literature, theater, or other so-called cultural pursuits. His only serious hobby was bridge. Although he joined practically every club open to him, he did not participate in club activities. His philosophy was almost anti-intellectual. He was a pragmatist who tended to distrust an academic or theoretical approach. Marvin Bower observed: "McKinsey was not a theorist, but he believed strongly in principles because he believed that only principles can be transferred from one situation to another. He was a very practical person."[43]

Although McKinsey never created a school of management thought, he did leave his mark upon those who worked closely with him. The tone of their respect and admiration for McKinsey is caught in comments made by Marvin Bower:

McKinsey was a great person and a great teacher. He believed in personal coaching, and that meant really telling a person about his mistakes and his opportunities to improve. He was rigorous but fair. I liked him, admired him, and respected him. My feeling for the man is shown by the fact that when our third son was born shortly after Mac's death, we named him James McKinsey Bower.[44]

Notes

1. Interview, February 16, 1973. Professor Newman studied with McKinsey at the University of Chicago. He worked as a consultant in McKinsey's firm and was McKinsey's staff assistant at Marshall Field and Company.

2. Ibid.

3. John G. Neukom, *McKinsey Memoirs: A Personal Perspective* (n.p.: John Neukom, 1957), p. 3. This is a personalized history of the firm founded by McKinsey. It is Neukom's summation of the development of the firm as well as a cursory biography of its founder.

4. James O. McKinsey, *Federal Income and Excess Profits Tax Laws* (Cincinnati, South-Western Publishing Co., 1920).

5. James O. McKinsey and A. C. Hodges, *Principles of Accounting* (Chicago: University of Chicago Press, 1920).

6. James O. McKinsey, *Bookkeeping and Accounting* (Cincinnati: South-Western Publishing Co., 1920). McKinsey published revised editions in 1926 and 1931. Further revised editions were published by Edwin Piper in 1938, 1939, and 1950.

7. James O. McKinsey, *Budgetary Control* (New York: Ronald Press, 1922).

8. McKinsey, *Bookkeeping and Accounting,* 2d ed. rev., p. 3. Emphasis added.

9. Ibid., p. 4.

10. This monograph was part of the special materials for the study of business developed at the University of Chicago. It was designed to facilitate teaching business by discussion methods. James O. McKinsey, *Cases*

and Problems No. 3, Organization and Methods of the Walworth Manufacturing Company (Chicago: University of Chicago Press, 1922).

11. James O. McKinsey, *Financial Management, an Outline of Its Principles and Problems*, 2 vols. (Chicago: American Technical Society, 1922). When this two-volume work was later revised and published as one volume it was with Willard J. Graham, a professor of accounting at the University of Chicago, as coauthor.

12. There is some question as to where McKinsey got his ideas — what their source was and how they evolved. There is evidence that he was influenced significantly by George Frazer. First, Frazer was his professor at the University of Chicago; second, Frazer hired him; third, Frazer said that McKinsey's book *Budgetary Control* pleased him because it followed outlines discussed in his seminar at the university in 1917 and 1918. Neukom, *McKinsey Memoirs*, p. 7.

13. Carl Heyel, ed., *Encyclopedia of Management* (New York: Litton Educational Publishing, 1963), pp. 527–28.

14. Leon P. Alford, "Ten Years Progress in Management, 1922–1933," in *Some Classic Contributions to Professional Managing: Historical Perspectives*, vol. 2 (n.p.: General Electric Co., 1956), p. 341.

15. Harry A. Hopf, "Soundings in the Literature of Management," in *Some Classic Contributions to Professional Managing: Historical Perspectives*, vol. 2 (n.p.: General Electric Co., 1956), pp. 501–2.

16. James O. McKinsey and Stuart P. Meech, *Controlling the Finances of a Business* (New York: Ronald Press, 1923).

17. Interview, February 16, 1973. Professor Newman is referring to Charles W. Gerstenberg, *Materials of Corporate Finance*.

18. James O. McKinsey, *Business Administration* (Cincinnati: South-Western Publishing Co., 1924).

19. James O. McKinsey, *Managerial Accounting*, vol. 1 (Chicago: University of Chicago Press, 1924).

20. McKinsey, *Business Administration*, p. 304.

21. McKinsey, *Managerial Accounting*, p. xiii.

22. McKinsey, *Business Administration*, p. 216.

23. L. P. Alford, ed., *Management's Handbook* (New York: Ronald Press, 1924), pp. 1269–1314.

24. L. C. Marshall, cited in James O. McKinsey, *Managerial Accounting*, pp. vii–ix.

25. Interview with John Neukom, October 3, 1975.

26. Interview, August 15, 1972. Professor Goetz was a student of McKinsey's at the University of Chicago. He also worked for McKinsey's consulting firm.

27. Interview, February 16, 1973.

28. Interview, October 3, 1975.

29. James O. McKinsey, *Accounting Principles* (Cincinnati: South-Western Publishing Co., 1929).

30. *American Business*, January 1938, p. 9. Reprinted by permission of *American Business*, Geyer-McAllister Publications, New York, New York.

31. William H. Newman, *Business Policies and Management* (Cincinnati: South-Western Publishing Co., 1940).

32. William H. Newman and James P. Logan, *Strategy, Policy and Central Management* (Cincinnati, Ohio: South-Western Publishing Co., 1976).

33. Interview, February 16, 1973.

34. Newman and Logan, *Strategy,* p. vi.

35. Interview, October 3, 1975.

36. Interview, February 16, 1973.

37. Correspondence, December 14, 1976. After McKinsey's death the strategy of McKinsey and Company was changed to include problem implementation.

38. Interview, February 16, 1973.

39. Interview, August 15, 1972.

40. Interview, October 3, 1975.

41. Interview, February 16, 1973.

42. Letter of July 20, 1936, quoted by Marvin Bower in correspondence, August 31, 1977.

43. Interview with Marvin Bower, director of the New York office of McKinsey and Company, conducted by Michael McManus on April 11, 1973.

44. Correspondence, August 31, 1977. Marvin Bower joined McKinsey and Company in 1933, and worked closely with McKinsey on a number of studies including the one for Marshall Field. Bower, managing director of McKinsey and Company from 1950 to 1967, is still associated with the firm.

Chapter II

McKinsey on Management

The goal of this chapter is to present the essence of McKinsey's thinking about management. It does so by examining his treatment of the management processes of organizing, directing, and controlling.[1]

A Perspective for Managers and Management Consultants

Anyone concerned with management should put it in perspective by seeing it in relation to other aspects of the world. Without such a broad view, a sense of proportion is lost and one might readily focus on treating symptoms rather than curing diseases. McKinsey recognized this, and in his writing he pointed to the fact that one has to see the organization as a whole. Moreover, he felt that the job of managing could not be viewed narrowly as just that of running an organization, but had to be seen in a larger context of politics and social issues. In modern parlance, this view of business organizations comes under the heading of "open systems theory." That is, the business organization is conceptualized as a system of interdependent parts functioning in a larger system. To be successful, executives must monitor and study the external forces which can influence their organization. As McKinsey said, "Administration is as much an external profession as an internal one."[2]

The complexity of an open systems approach to business management must be emphasized. Where everything is related to everything else, simple cause-and-effect reasoning is specious. The manager and the consultant must grasp the whole. They must see or sense the relationships. They need a strategy for understanding and managing this complexity. They must constantly be aware of the fact that "each element of administration is dependent on each of the other [elements]."[3]

A Strategy for the Study of Business Administration

Once the problem of understanding business administration[4] — that is, the need to develop a general perspective emphasizing interdependencies, synthesis, and relations with the broader society — is recognized, the question becomes how to study administration without being confused and overwhelmed. The difficulty in dealing with this question increases greatly when one takes McKinsey's position that organizations have to be differentiated from each other, and the practices of management need to be designed to fit each firm's special problems.

McKinsey's answer was to separate those activities which occur in all managerial settings — the processes of management — from the specialized functions that tend to be found in every business organization: marketing, production, finance, personnel, purchasing, traffic, and controllership. Thus, he started by isolating the essence of management. McKinsey recognized that analyzing the functional areas, such as marketing and production, of a business as separate and distinct entities is artificial. However, he rationalized his approach as follows: "This assumption [of functional specialization] has greatly facilitated our discussion of administration for it has made possible a consideration of business activities in terms of homogeneous groups. Without such a grouping of business activities their discussion would be an endless task."[5]

One point that should be emphasized is that in his discussion of functional areas of management, McKinsey always advised that each organization is unique and one must shape policies and strategies according to the specific environment in which they are to be applied.

The Management Processes

In his writings McKinsey usually used the term *administrator* rather than *manager*.[6] The central goal of the administrator is "to make a product of value to the human race and a profit to the producers."[7] To do this, the administrator must perform the management processes; that is, he must formulate plans, establish procedures for implementing them, and provide controls to see that they are carried out. In contemporary management literature this is known as the process school of management. According to this school, the process of management involves (1) organizing — planning and deciding what is to be done; (2) directing — deciding and communicating how it is to be done, and (3) controlling — establishing procedures and techniques to

Figure 1.   McKinsey's Analytical Framework for Understanding Management

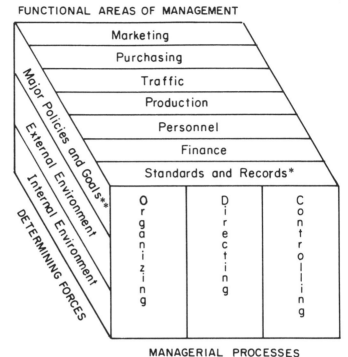

FUNCTIONAL AREAS OF MANAGEMENT

MANAGERIAL PROCESSES

*In his early writings, McKinsey treated standards and records as a functional area of management. In later years he treated these as a managerial process of controlling.

**McKinsey's discussion of policies can be confusing. He was not consistent in differentiating major policies, such as products and markets, from operating policies. Operating policies are management processes, whereas major policies are determining forces.

ensure what is organized and directed is actually accomplished.[8] McKinsey also described the common activities involved in carrying out the management processes as: (1) establishing major policies; (2) planning and setting up an organization for carrying out these policies; and (3) operating or running the organization, which involves establishing and enforcing operating procedures.[9] Thus, in studying administration, one can focus on the major policies of the firm, the formal organization structure, and the operating procedures. In essence, this involves studying the manner in which the various activities are organized, directed, and controlled.

The management processes are carried on for the organization as a whole and for each of its significant parts. It is by arbitrarily isolating the common management processes and assuming a functional organization structure that McKinsey simplified the essence of management sufficiently to provide a rudimentary grasp of the subject.

The framework suggested by McKinsey can be viewed as a three-dimensional matrix (see figure 1) which can be used to analyze any firm. It views each funtional area of management such as production, finance, or personnel as being managed: organized, directed, and controlled. But in each setting unique aspects of management will be determined by major policies and internal and external forces.

The first step in summarizing the essentials of McKinsey on management is to see how he treated the general processes of management: organizing, directing, and controlling.

Organizing

McKinsey's treatment of organizing centered on the process of planning. For him, planning included the establishment of major policies. He defined a policy as "a plan of action based upon assumed conditions."[10] Moreover, he saw planning as the natural result of analyzing relevant facts logically. He emphasized that "plans are no better than the knowledge upon which they are based."[11]

In the formulations of plans McKinsey maintained an open systems perspective. He suggested that top executives keep abreast of economic conditions. To this end he suggested that the following indexes be examined.[12]

1. Stock and bond prices
2. Unfilled steel orders, pig iron production, and prices
3. The condition, yield, and prices of the principal crops, such as wheat, cotton, and corn
4. Banking indexes
   a. Bank clearing outside of New York
   b. The ratio of reserves to note and deposit liabilities for the commercial banking system as a whole
   c. Ratio of loans to deposits in New York
   d. Interest rates
   e. The flow of gold
5. Foreign trade and exchange rates
6. Labor conditions
7. Railroad conditions
8. Business failures

9. New building
10. Price indexes
11. Social and political factors such as war and tariffs[13]

Of course, the economy has changed considerably since 1923 when McKinsey drew up his list of indexes. Today we would use many additional measures, such as the Gross National Product and other specially constructed statistical indexes, but the important point McKinsey made is that the successful executive must continually make plans in tune with a constantly changing and dynamic business environment.

Moreover, the forecaster must use these indexes with discretion: they should not be taken at face value. The essence of successful forecasting is carefully thinking out how changes in specific indexes might affect the executive's organization. The successful forecaster constantly relates practically everything he encounters to his business.[14] Such things as price changes, changes in dividend policies, and wage advances influence forecasts. Ultimately the forecaster weighs and evaluates the data he has available, putting them into perspective with the unique forces operating in his firm. This involves sound judgment.[15]

In his later years, McKinsey taught business policy, concentrating on the formation of broad plans of action. In 1932, he gave a paper at the American Management Association General Management Conference on "Adjusting Policies to Meet Changing Conditions," in which he dealt with some of the essential issues in planning and policy thinking. He considered policies important because they force management to anticipate problems and in so doing develop intelligent lines of action. They allow those who have a broader perspective of the firm and the right knowledge, rather than those with a narrow view, to set guidelines. Policies also tend to expedite action and to give some uniformity to the actions of all the members of the organization. The existence of policies also gives management a standard by which to judge the actions of members of the organization. Finally, policies tend to ensure continuity of action and greater predictability of organization behavior.

With respect to policies, McKinsey specifically warned that conditions change and policies need to be adapted to meet them. A review of business history shows that changes commonly occur in (1) products produced,

(2) methods of production, (3) methods of distribution, and (4) general economic activities.

It is essential for the executive to develop good judgment, and this implies adopting a research point of view. McKinsey called this "intelligent and common sense research." A research point of view "emphasizes the urgent necessity for contrast, and intelligent study of the past and present as a means of anticipating the future." McKinsey went on to state that "the executive must not be a slave to tradition; must not be closed-minded, must not believe that what has been must continue to be or that what is different from what he has been accustomed to cannot be right."[16]

In summary, top management policies need to be based on facts, to change to meet changing conditions, and to coordinate the specialized activities of the organization. Successful policies are the result of analytical thinking, synthesis, and sound judgment.

Directing

The general processes of management are interdependent. Organizing as a process implies directing, directing implies organizing, and both imply controlling. They are like separate legs of a three-legged stool. Each leg can be analyzed, but for the stool to stand, each leg has to be in proper relation to the others. Bearing this interdependence in mind, we can abstract and analyze directing, where we deal with the formal structure of the firm. The need for a formal organization should be obvious. "Without formal organization we have uncoordinated, undirected activities, from which satisfactory results cannot be expected."[17]

The starting place for considering the formal organizational structure is the recognition that it is uniquely determined in each firm. Each firm adjusts to accommodate its size, types of operations, personnel, and location of units. It is dangerous to generalize about structure. Nevertheless, we can point to some precepts and caveats regarding the design of organizations. These center on policies relating to control, responsibility, authority, span of control, and the like.[18]

Requisites for Good Organizational Stucture. The following requisites for good organizational structure are applicable to all forms of organizations.

1. "In every oganization there should be centralized control. This means that the organization as a whole as well as

each division of the organization should have an executive head who has final authority over the activities under his jurisdiction."[19]

2. "Good organization necessitates that definite responsibility be fixed for making all decisions which can be anticipated, ... not only should responsibility be fixed for the making of decisions but equally responsibility should be fixed for their enforcement."[20]

3. "Final responsibility for executing decisions should be placed in an individual and not in a group."[21]

4. "A proper procedure for handling unusual problems should be established."[22]

5. "Authority should accompany responsibility."[23] For example, a branch manager who is held responsible for his unit must be given formal authority over those who assist him.[24]

6. "The number of subordinate executives reporting to each executive should be limited. The president or chief executive should usually have not more than five or six executives reporting to him."[25]

7. "Provision for specialization should be made." Specialization promotes efficiency and hence should be encouraged. At the same time it tends to divide the organization and complicate problems of coordination. McKinsey suggested using committees and budgetary control to help ensure coordination.[26]

8. A system of promotion should be provided from within. Such a system will help motivate individuals by ensuring that efficient performance is rewarded.[27]

9. Organizational structure represents a balance between the organization as an abstraction and the abilities and limitations of individuals. The structure should reflect the interests and capacities of the individuals who are members of the organization.[28] "Usually it is not possible to set up an ideal organization and then secure the men needed to fill the various positions in the organization."[29]

10. Line control should be distinguished from functional control: "Generally speaking, an executive has line control over activities when he is responsible for the performance of these activities, and he has functional control over the activities when he is responsible for prescribing the method

by which these activities are performed or has the authority of approving the method by which they are performed.... The authority of the personnel manager and of the controller is largely functional."[30] Furthermore, line authority should be distinguished from staff authority: "A staff man is one who exercises *no* authority to prescribe how activities are to be performed. He is simply one who studies, carries on research, analyzes problems and presents the results of his studies with his recommendations, to a line man who may or may not accept these recommendations."[31]

11. In most instances, an organization chart should be drawn up. In the process, all the activities that need to be performed will be ascertained and classified on some logical basis. "An organization chart is merely an administrative device which enables an executive to see the men who are responsible for performing the activities of the company."[32]

12. Maintaining an organization chart is a continuing process. Conditions change and the formal structure of the organization should reflect such changes. Moreover, "there is no one kind of organization chart that is right. ... Every business has to work out its own organization in terms of its particular problems and personnel."[33]

Conclusion. These precepts for designing the formal structure of an organization are based on McKinsey's writings in the 1920s, and thus precede many of the classic articles and concepts of today. Yet conceptually they are in tune with the process school of management thought as developed by Harold Koontz, Cyril O'Donnell, and Henri Fayol, among others. In essence, McKinsey held that formal organization structure needs to be tailored to the special problems and unique situation of each firm; that structure must be as dynamic and changing as the world it reflects; that the essence of structure is specialization and division of labor, which produces problems of coordination and integration; that the span of executive control should be limited; that responsibility should be clearly delineated; that authority and responsibility should go together; that line and functional control should be differentiated, that line authority should be treated differently from staff authority; and that organization charts are useful management devices. In his own way, McKinsey covered what later appeared as Graicunas's theory of span of control;[34] Mooney and Reiley's scalar process, which Koontz and O'Donnell identify as the chain of command;[35] Fayol's principles of (1) division of work, (2) authority and responsibility, (3) unity of command, and (4) unity of direction;[36] and aspects of what has become known as contingency theory.[37]

Controlling

Controlling, the third process of management, involves developing procedures and techniques to accomplish what has been planned. Before discussing the dynamics of McKinsey's treatment of controlling, it is desirable to repeat that plannning, organizing, and controlling are closely interrelated. Each determines and is determined by the others. For example, the design of an organizational structure influences planning and control both implicitly and explicitly.

McKinsey's philosophy of management centered on the control process. His book on budgeting still stands as a classic in the field, and his early work in management focused on managerial applications of bookkeeping and accounting as tools in decision making and control.

The Budgeting System. The central thrust of McKinsey's work on control is the use of "the budgetary idea as a basic managerial tool *useful* in efficient management." To him, "the budget idea is very simple.... [It] is just ordinary common sense applied to the management of a business." McKinsey described the budget idea as follows: "You study what you have done, you think about what you are going to do, you formulate plans as a basis of this study and then finally you set up a proper organization to carry out these plans and see that this organization functions."[38]

The easiest way to present McKinsey's approach to budgeting is to describe in his own words how it operates.

The procedure to be followed by a business firm in the installation and operation of budgetary control will of necessity vary, depending primarily on the organization of the business and the nature of its operations. A possible procedure, stated briefly and in outline form, is as follows:

1. Each department prepares an estimate of its activities for the budget period. The method of stating these activites depends on the nature of the operations of the department, the sales department stating the sales it expects to make and the estimated expenses it will incur in making these sales; the production department stating the estimated production for the period and the estimated requirements in

materials, labor, and manufacturing expenses to meet this estimate; the service departments, such as the personnel department, the traffic department, the accounting department, and the office manager's department, stating the estimated expenditures of their departments. Because of the interdependence of these departments, some will need to use the estimates of other departments in making their own estimates. For instance, the production department must know the estimated sales before it can estimate the production necessary to meet the sales demands; the treasurer must know the plans of all the departments before he can estimate his cash receipts and cash disbursements. Consequently a procedure must be set up which provides for a proper scheduling of the estimates with reference to preparation and distribution.

2.   The departmental heads will transmit the departmental estimates to an executive who has supervision of the budgetary procedure. Sometimes the controller acts in this capacity, while in many cases the duty is delegated to a member of the staff of the general manager or president. Since many businesses do not have a controller, it will be assumed during the present discussion that an assistant to the president acts in this capacity. This official combines the estimates of all the departments into a proposed financial budget for the business. In preparing this estimate he will be assisted by the treasurer, though in some cases this budget is prepared by the treasurer alone. The proposed financial budget should show the estimated receipts from all sources and the estimated expenditures by all departments of the business.

3.   The executive in charge of the budget procedure makes a comparison between the estimated receipts and the estimated expenditures as shown by the proposed budget. If the estimated expenditures exceed the estimated receipts, one of the following courses of action must be taken:

a.   The departmental expenditures may be reduced. In making such reductions a problem arises due to the fact that the reduction of expenditures may result in a reduction of receipts. For instance, if the expenditures of the advertising department are reduced, this may result in a reduction of sales, with a consequent reduction of receipts from collections. In the same manner, a reduction of the expenditures of the production department may result in a reduction of production, with a consequent lack of goods to meet sales demands which will result in a reduction of receipts from sales. Care must be taken, therefore, in the reduction of expenditures to see that receipts are not reduced more than proportionately.

b.   Additional receipts may be secured. It may be possible by speeding up operations and securing more efficient administration to secure additional receipts without incurring a proportionate increase of expenditures.

c.   Additional capital may be secured. If it is not deemed wise to reduce expenditures, plans must be made to secure additional capital with which to finance the excess of expenditures over receipts. It is understood, of course, that this condition cannot continue for long, otherwise the business will find it necessary to liquidate.

The executive in charge of the budgetary procedure may make recommendations with reference to possible procedures, but he is usually not invested with authority to determine the plans to be followed.

4. The executive in charge of the budgetary procedure prepares from the departmental estimates an estimated balance sheet and an estimated statement of profit and loss, showing respectively the anticipated financial condition at the end of the budget period and the anticipated result of the operations of the period.

5. The departmental estimates, together with the proposed financial budget, and the estimated financial statements, are submitted by the executive in charge of the budgetary procedure to a budget committee, composed of the principal executives of the company and presided over by the president. This committee considers the proposed estimates and makes such revisions as it thinks necessary. In case the proposed budgets involve important changes in the company's policy, or require the securing of additional capital for a material amount, it may be necessary to submit them to the board of directors for consideration. Indeed, in some businesses all budgetary plans are submitted to the board of directors for approval. After the proposed estimates have been approved, they constitute the working program for the budget period. The budgets as adopted set limits upon the expenditures of all the departments, and these limits cannot be exceeded without the permission of the budget committee. The budgets also set up standards of performance for certain departments. For instance, the sales budget states the sales that are to be made by the sales department, and the production budget states the estimated production of the production department.

6. Each department makes plans which will enable it to carry out its program as outlined by its budget. For instance, the advertising department makes contracts for advertising space; the sales department sets quotas for its salesmen; the production department sets up schedules of production.

7. Records are established so that the performance of each department may be properly recorded and comparisons made between the estimated and the actual performance. Periodic reports, showing a comparison between the estimated and the actual performance of each department for the budget period, are made to the executive in charge of the budgetary procedure and are by him transmitted to the budget committee and in some cases to the board of directors. On the basis of these reports the budget committee or board of directors may make such revisions of the budgetary program as it may deem desirable.

The foregoing procedure is intended to be suggestive only. Each organization must adopt a procedure which is fitted to its particular needs. The purpose of the foregoing outline is to indicate what budgetary control is by suggesting how it operates. From this outline it can be seen that budgetary control involves the following:

1. The statement of the plans of all the departments of the business for a certain period of time in the form of estimates.

2. The coordination of these estimates into a well-balanced program for the business as a whole.

3. The preparation of reports showing a comparison between the actual and the estimated performance, and the revision of the original plans when these reports show that such a revision is necessary.[39]

As can be seen, determining standards or reference points for measuring is a critical aspect of budgeting. For McKinsey, "a standard is an expression of (a) the desired method of performing an activity or (b) the desired or expected result from the performance of an activity or group of activities."[40] Although it is difficult to classify standards we can, for the purpose of discussion, consider three broad types: (1) standard procedures, (2) financial standards, and (3) operating standards.

Standard procedures are instructions to various units of an organization specifying how things should be done and to whom information should be reported. They are essential for coordinated operations. For example, when a sales department receives an order it must know that the customer has adequate credit, that the goods are available, and that the goods can be shipped and delivered according to the customer's needs. Hence, standard procedures need to be established to ensure coordination and prevent conflicts.

With respect to standard procedures, McKinsey made two basic rules:

1. "Standard procedures should be developed and operated under supervision of a central authority."[41] This is essential for coordination and efficiency. Without a central authority, specialized areas are apt to pursue their respective interests without consideration of other aspects of the firm.

2. Standard procedures should be in written form. This tends to prevent misunderstandings and ensure continuity when personnel changes.[42]

Financial standards supplement the usual reports such as the balance sheet or profit and loss statement. They express relationships in terms of ratios, such as the following commonly used ones:

1. Borrowed capital to total capital.
2. Owned capital to total capital.
3. Each kind of asset to total assets.
4. Current assets to current liabilities.
5. Borrowed capital to the cost of capital.
6. Net profit to total capital.
7. Net profit to net worth.
8. Gross sales to gross profits.
9. Sales to net profits.
10. Sales to inventories
11. Sales to accounts receivable.
12. Sales to fixed assets.
13. Sales to total assets.
14. Costs and expenses to sales.
15. Average inventory to cost of goods sold.[43]

McKinsey emphasized that these ratios are only suggestive. They are meant to be developed as standards for specific firms, and as such they need to be compared with other firms in similar industries or some other reference point. Where meaningful comparisons can be made, the ratios become measures for judging efficiency.

Operating standards refers to standards which are not necessarily available from normal accounting procedures, such as the balance sheet or profit and loss statement. They include performance standards, credit standards, quality standards, and the like, and they may be expressed in other than financial form.

In any specific firm, the form and nature of standards have to be designed to fit existing circumstances. Despite this, certain common guides help in establishing a good program:

1. The standard should be as simple as possible. This is especially applicable to standard procedures, as complex procedures tend to encourage errors and decrease efficiency.

2. A standard should be comprehensive and flexible enough to fit most conditions. "Variations in normal routines are necessary in most firms and authorized procedures should be sufficiently flexible to provide for these."[44]

3. Standards should be kept up to date; they should be adaptable to changing conditions.

4: A standard should be determined by careful, systematic

investigation, not by guesswork or haphazard methods.

5.   A standard should be stated in terms that will facilitate comparisons between actual and standard performance.[45]

In summary, McKinsey saw standards as devices to encourage systematic, "scientific" study of what is being done so that realistic reference points can be established to evaluate and control it. Although the procedure sounds mechanistic and automatic, McKinsey recognized that precise standardization is seldom possible; hence, he advocated that procedures and practices be accommodated to changing conditions and he highlighted exceptions. In this manner, the executive receives good feedback and can be alert to emergency situations as well as evolving trends.

Budgeting and the Processes of Management. Although our emphasis has been on budgeting as a control device, it is important to point out that to McKinsey a budgeting system was almost synonymous with management. It ensured the essentials of efficient and effective management in that it provided:

1.   Planning. Budgeting requires a systematic collection of data that can be used to understand the past and predict the future.

2.   Policy thinking and understanding of policies throughout the organization. McKinsey succinctly stated: "A budget, in final analysis, is nothing more than a statement of the fundamental policies of the business."[46]

3.   Commitment of executives to their specialized tasks and to the overall organization. Effective budgeting requires executives in specialized areas to recognize the interdependency of their departments and to work together to coordinate all parts of the business. Moreover, the budgeting procedure advocated by McKinsey "starts with the men in the organization who are responsible for carrying out the budget."[47] Thus, the procedure starts at the lower levels of the organization and offers men in the field an opportunity to have a voice in the management of the business.[48]

4.   Anticipating problems and presenting many of the most important problems for solution. Harold Geneen of the International Telegraph and Telephone Company, one of the most widely recognized management practitioners,

has the motto: "no surprises." This is an essential by-product of the procedures McKinsey advocated, and it means that management is successfully maintaining the organization and adjusting it to changing conditions.[49]

5. Evaluating peformance. The end result of a good budgeting system is knowledge of how the firm and each department are progressing. It is measurement based on realistic standards and study rather than past history. Thus, budgeting becomes a way to identify excellence in performance, spot weaknesses, and take corrective actions.

Administration of Budgeting. McKinsey saw budgeting in a "contingency" framework; namely, budgeting systems had to be tailor-made for each company. "There are no standard methods or procedures which have general application in the installation and operation of budgets. . . . The form to be used in budgetary procedure should always be designed for the special needs of each company."[50] Despite the uniqueness of each budgeting system, McKinsey did suggest some general guides for those installing and administrating a budgetary system. He emphasized that the firm should work out its budgeting procedure before focusing on departmental estimates. Important aspects of procedures involve:

1. Length of the budgeting period. This is a function of variables such as merchandise turnover, production cycle, finances, accounting period, and market conditions. All departments need to be aware of the period involved so that realistic comparisons may be made and all budgets coordinated.

2. Responsibility for preparation of estimates. A number of estimates are required for a budgeting system, and McKinsey held that "as a general rule better results will be obtained if the individuals responsible for the performance of the estimate are the ones who originate it."[51]

3. Responsibility for reports and for reporting. Once budgets are set, it is important to confirm what is actually happening. This involves determining the kind of reports to be prepared as well as to whom they go. McKinsey believed that it was best to have a central authority design the budget reports in order to coordinate various parts of the organization. In this way, reports would be in the proper form for comparison and correlations. The executive in charge of

budget procedure should know the form of information desired for the use of the departments and the budget committee.[52]

4.   Promptness in preparing reports. As an instrument of control, budget reports have to be available as close to the end of the reporting period as possible. For this reason, McKinsey advised that it was best to avoid, wherever possible, having the accounting department prepare budget reports, since in his experience that department seldom rendered reports with sufficient speed.[53]

5.   Methods of enforcing budgets. The budgeting idea not only involves establishing standards and goals, but also formulating plans to carry out estimates. Hence, McKinsey advocated a well-thought-out plan for attaining and enforcing departmental estimates. Such things as sales quotas and balance of stores records are necessary to ensure that the budget is maintained.

6.   A manual of budgetary procedures. Part of the success of a budgeting system arises from the fact that its procedures are clearly laid out. This means that for each firm a manual of budgetary procedure should be written. It should specify the organizational structure — such as the role of the officers, the budget committee, and so forth — and the procedures for dealing with interdepartmental relationships arising from the budgetary program. The manual should be aimed at all executives and hence not weighted with detailed department specifications.

McKinsey's illustration of a manual of budgeting procedures (Appendix B) begins by identifying strategic factors related to the firm to which the manual applies. The manual itself helps in developing understanding and suggests a format that can be adapted for use by other firms.[54]

Of central importance in budgeting procedures is the requirement that all departmental estimates be submitted to the budget committee at one time; that they be considered and approved within two days after their receipt; and that immediately after their approval, the estimates be returned to department heads. The need for this requirement arises from the interdependence of departmental budgets and the need for central control of all the activities of the business. "For instance, the production department cannot prepare the finished goods estimate until it receives the sales estimate; the purchasing department cannot prepare the estimate of purchases until it receives the estimate of materials requirements; and the assistant to the general manager cannot prepare the estimated financial statements until he receives all estimates."[55]

7. Decentralized responsibility, centralized control.[56] While it is true that those at lower levels in the organization should be consulted regarding the budgets relative to their responsibilities, it is also true that they cannot do an adequate job unless they have information as to the plans of the company and have formulated plans for their own units. This means that upper- and lower-echelon executives need to harmonize their plans.

Budgeting must therefore be recognized as more than a flow of data, for it also involves educating the organization about policies and plans. This in turn implies committee activity, where people from different areas of the organization discuss and harmonize their budgets. "If this is done the general budget committee, composed of the major executives of the business, will, in fact, become the policy-making agency of the company. Unless this committee does function in this way, budgets are likely to become only additional red tape."[57] The lower levels in the organization will not understand what is going on and top management will establish budgets arbitrarily without adequate data. In short, lower-level executives should be given the information they need to plan for their units and to establish their own budget estimates. This involves delegating responsibility. But controls need to be centralized in order to coordinate the units of the business. Hence, the budget committee is essential and it needs to function as a forum for open discussion, for disseminating information about plans of lower-level units and for the business as a whole, and as a decision-making body for policies and budgets.[58]

Conclusion. This discussion of McKinsey's approach to control has concentrated on budgetary control. It abstracted from McKinsey's discussion of budgets in functional areas such as sales, production, and personnel in order to avoid being overwhelmed by details. Throughout the discussion, emphasis has been on general procedures and guides to practitioners to the point where we risk losing a proper perspective on budgeting. Budgets are merely administrative devices, "no more efficient than the organization and management which uses them."[59]

McKinsey's view on the limitations of budgets is captured in his remarks to a symposium on budgeting technique presented at the annual convention of the American Management Association in 1926. "I hope that you do not go away with the feeling that the budget is a panacea for all ills, or that by itself it will solve all problems, but you should realize that a budget is an administrative device and is no better than the organization which makes it and no better than the organization which carries it out. The budget is not a substitute for good management, or for good policies, or for good organization. It is but a device which can be used to promote all of these."[60]

In his writings McKinsey touched upon only a few budgeting problems: (1) it takes considerable time to install a budget and make it work; (2) subordinates may attempt to pad their salaries and costs to protect their showing against "the budget"; and (3) red tape may hinder efficiency.[61] He neglected the problems arising when tyranny and fear dominate the budget committee, when executives feel insecure and under pressure to protect their flanks, and when budgets are manipulated for personal ends. Of course, these are not budget problems per se, but problems of the organization which are expressed and manifested in the budgetary procedures. Perhaps they are insoluble, in which case budgeting systems must always be less than perfect. In fact, McKinsey advised: "Don't expect that you will ever have a perfect budget for you probably never will. But I desire to leave you with this last thought — isn't it better to plan ahead and think ahead, even though those plans are only approximately correct than not to plan at all?"[62]

Notes

1. What I have done is to summarize and interpret the central ideas that appear in McKinsey's writings. It should be recognized at the outset that, although my goal is to summarize, I cannot separate myself from myself; thus the materials may be subjected to selective perception and other biases. I have tried to avoid this danger by quoting frequently, cross-referencing, and otherwise going back to source data. But errors can creep in. Further, my goal is to present a useful framework for viewing management as well as a summary of McKinsey's ideas. Thus, I have taken some liberty in my form of presentation by trying to avoid mechanical summaries and occasionally putting the ideas in my own idiom.

2. James O. McKinsey, *Sixteen Trends in Management Organization,* Annual Convention Series, no. 33 (New York: American Management Association, 1926), p. 22.

3. McKinsey, *Business Administration,* p. 13.

4. Marvin Bower recalls: "Mac used 'administration' as synonymous

with 'managing,'" but Bower believes that today "Mac would recognize that there is a valid distinction between these terms, with administration dealing more with carrying out strategy and policies which are ingredients of managing." Correspondence, August 31, 1977.

5. McKinsey, *Business Administration,* p. 277.

6. There is reason to believe that today McKinsey would distinguish between managing and administration. See footnote 4.

7. McKinsey, *Business Administration,* p. 216.

8. See McKinsey, *Business Administration,* pp. 12 14. See also Robert Tannenbaum, "The Management Concept, A Rational Synthesis," *Journal of Business* 22 (October 1949): 232 – 41.

9. McKinsey, *Businesss Administration,* p. 12.

10. James O. McKinsey, *Adjusting Policies to Meet Changing Conditions,* General Management Series, no. 116 (New York: American Management Association, 1932), p. 3.

11. James O. McKinsey, *Budgeting Technique,* Annual Convention Series, no. 51 (New York: American Management Association, 1926), p. 75.

12. McKinsey and Meech, *Controlling the Finances of a Business,* pp. 17 – 19.

13. Ibid., pp. 26 – 37.

14. Ibid., p. 33.

15. Ibid., p. 36.

16. McKinsey, *Adjusting Policies,* pp. 8 – 9.

17. McKinsey, *Business Administration,* p. 277.

18. Ibid., p. 282.

19. Ibid., p. 283.

20. Ibid.

21. Ibid.

22. Ibid.

23. Ibid.

24. McKinsey did not analyze responsibility or authority; for example, he did not differentiate formal from informal authority or the sources of authority. Nor did he delve into the essence of responsibility — what it is, how it is delegated, and so forth. Thus, he took a simplistic position in which responsibility is usually synonymous with "accountability," rather than the moral aspects of an individual's sense of "responsibility."

25. McKinsey, *Business Administration,* pp. 284 – 85.

26. Ibid., p. 285.

27. Ibid.

28. McKinsey, *Business Administration,* p. 280.

29. McKinsey, "Sixteen Trends," p. 13.

30. Ibid., p. 11.

31. Ibid., p. 12.

32. Ibid., p. 23.

33. Ibid.

34. A. V. Graicunas, "Relationships in Organization," in *Papers on the Science of Administration,* ed. Luther Gulick and Lyndall F. Urwick (New York: Institute of Public Administration, Columbia University, 1937), pp. 183 – 87.

35. James D. Mooney and Alan C. Reiley, *Onward Industry* (New York: Harper and Bros., 1931). Later revised as *The Principles of Organization* (New York: Harper and Bros., 1939), then revised by James Mooney in 1947. Harold Koontz and Cyril O'Donnell, *Principles of Management,* 4th ed. (New York: McGraw-Hill, 1968). This book is probably the largest-selling text in the field. It was first published in 1955 and to a significant degree it parallels McKinsey's concepts. Cyril O'Donnell received his Ph.D. in business administration at the University of Chicago while McKinsey was teaching there.

36. Henri Fayol, *General and Industrial Management,* trans. Constance Storrs (London: Sir Isaac Pitman and Sons, Ltd., 1949). Fayol gave several papers in French but his work was not available in English until 1929, when the International Management Institute at Geneva, Switzerland, published a translation by J. A. Corbrough. One of Fayol's papers was available in English in 1923 — "The Administrative Theory in the State," translated by Sarah Greer — and appeared in the collection edited by Gulick and Urwick cited in footnote 34.

37. I associated contingency theory with the work of Paul Lawrence and Jay Lorsch at the Harvard Business School. See Paul R. Lawrence and Jay W. Lorsch, *Organization and Environment: Managing Differentiation and Integration* (Boston: Division of Research, Harvard Graduate School of Business Administration, 1967.)

In recent years *contingency* has tended to replace *systems* as the popular terminology in management texts. See, for example, Don Hellriegel and John W. Slocum, Jr., *Management: A Contingency Approach* (Reading, Mass.: Addison-Wesley Publishing Co., 1974); Fremont E. Kast and James E. Rosenzweig, *Contingency View of Organization and Management* (Chicago: Science Research Associates, 1973); and Gary Dessler, *Organization and Management: A Contingency Approach* (Englewood Cliffs, N.J.: Prentice-Hall, 1976). In essence, a contingency approach to management appears to be an elaboration of the position taken by many management theorists. For example, see Mary Parker Follett's comments regarding "the law of the situation," in *Dynamic Administration,* ed. Henry C. Metcalf and Lyndall F. Urwick (New York: Harper and Bros., 1940), p. 58; William B. Wolf, "Organizational Constructs. An Approach to Understanding Organizations," *Journal of the Academy of Management* 1, no. 1 (April 1958): 7–15, also in *Current Issues and Emerging Concepts in Management,* ed. Dalton E. McFarland, vol. 2 (New York: Houghton Mifflin, 1966), pp. 185–94.

38. McKinsey, "Budgeting Technique," p. 68.

39. Reprinted from McKinsey, *Budgetary Control,* pp. 5–8. With respect to the above, Goetz observed that "McKinsey's was a zero-based budgeting which was a cost-benefit approach, and a complete anticipation of PPB (Programs, Planning, Budgeting)." Interview, August 15, 1972.

40. McKinsey, *Managerial Accounting,* p. 20.

41. Ibid., p. 23.

42. Ibid., p. 23–24.

43. Ibid., p. 27.

44. Ibid., p. 31.

45. Ibid.

46. McKinsey, *Budgeting Technique,* p. 72.

47. Ibid., p. 73.

48. Ibid., p. 74.

49. To a large extent, ITT is an example of the application of some of the concepts McKinsey advanced.

50. James O. McKinsey and W. S. Clithero, *Successful Departmental Budgeting*, Annual Convention Series, no. 65 (New York: American Management Association, 1928), p. 13.

51. McKinsey, *Budgetary Control*, p. 37.

52. Ibid., pp. 38–39.

53. Ibid., p. 40.

54. Ibid., pp. 375–93.

55. Ibid., p. 394.

56. McKinsey and Clithero, *Successful Departmental Budgeting*, p. 15.

57. Ibid., p. 18.

58. To a large degree, McKinsey was advocating a system that today would be called management by objectives (MBO).

59. McKinsey and Clithero, *Successful Departmental Budgeting*, p. 19.

60. McKinsey, *Budgeting Technique*, Annual Convention Series, no. 51. (New York: American Management Association, 1926), p. 75.

61. McKinsey, *Budgeting Technique*, p. 15.

62. Ibid., p. 76.

Chapter III

McKinsey the Consultant

James O. McKinsey ranks among the world's best consultants. Back in the 1920s he was charging five hundred dollars a day and getting more requests for his services than he could handle. Moreover, he founded the nucleus of two of today's eminent consulting firms: McKinsey and Company and A. T. Kearney and Company.[1]

How did McKinsey become a successful consultant? What did he do to attract and hold clients? Although all the subtleties of McKinsey's success can never be uncovered, highlighting some of his activities and ideas will help identify significant aspects of his success in consulting.

Career Strategy

Professional consulting was McKinsey's lifelong career goal. He had planned a strategy to achieve this end. He used to say that to be a successful consultant one needed three ingredients:

1. Unquestioned respectability
2. A reputation for expertise in an area of some concern to top management
3. Professional exposure[2]

McKinsey established his respectability through his academic connections, gained his reputation for expertise by his writings, and obtained professional exposure by working as a consultant for Frazer and Torbet and by numerous activities in business and civil life. John Neukom recalled that McKinsey "wrote a great deal and gave numerous speeches. . . . He believed very much in contribution to your community through the Red Cross, YMCA, AMA, and other groups because he thought it was part of being a good citizen. Night after night he was out making speeches on behalf of one or another organization. He worked damn hard at it."[3]

McKinsey systematically met and courted influential people. The following story told by Billy Goetz illustrates the lengths to which McKinsey would go:

I know that he moved to an apartment house in Chicago on Lake Shore Drive for one reason. The apartment had two units on each floor. When you got off the elevator, there were two doors. McKinsey wanted to meet the man behind the other door, so he rented the apartment next to his. On another occasion, he said that on every occasion he went to New York, he would buy a certain banker his lunch. He did this until after several dozen times he got his first assignment from the man. He got a great deal of work at the luncheon table.

McKinsey also devoted mealtimes to business; according to Goetz, he claimed to eat all his lunches, half his breakfasts, and a third of his dinners with clients or prospective clients.[4]

The importance of having meals with prospective clients or good contacts was elaborated on by John Neukom:

Mac had the idea that the lunch hour was a very important hour of the day and that it could be used effectively. This idea of sitting around talking about last Saturday's football game would drive him wild. He would have none of that sort of thing. He'd have a list of the people he wanted to have lunch with. Everyday he'd call until he found somebody who was free for lunch. He had a lunch with somebody to which there was a purpose. Maybe the purpose was to get new clients, maybe the purpose was to follow-up on some recommendations he had made, but there was always a purpose. It was not just a helter-skelter having nothing else to do so "let's have lunch" sort of thing. And Mac said many times that this is what we all ought to do. And many of us did it. He used the financial community. He said, "I have bought a lunch for every important banker in Chicago and New York at one time or another, and nearly every one at one time or another has given me some work. ..."

One time he said, "except one." This man was an executive in a New York bank. He said, "I have been courting him for several years and I have never gotten a nickel's worth of business and I can't understand why he is the exception." About six months later he came to the office one day. He used to walk up and down and drop in on people. He said: "I have completed the circle. Remember the guy from that New York bank? Well, I find out that he's the one who got us the XYZ Company study. I never knew how that happened. I never knew and always worried about this guy. Now I know."[5]

What did McKinsey talk about at these lunches? How did he handle himself? It is difficult to answer these questions, but in the course of querying many people who knew

McKinsey well, I received consistent answers. Walter McKinsey, a nephew who was close to McKinsey, said that his uncle "had the ability to gain the complete confidence of the person he was talking to and he did that without vacillating. . . . He didn't oversell or try to give the individual . . . any great privileges. . . . He wanted only facts."[6]

McKinsey's Style

Newman described how McKinsey related to people, and his description makes it clear why people chose McKinsey to solve their problems. According to Newman:

It was partly his humorous stories, but he quickly tried to find out what the other person was interested in and see if he couldn't help that other person resolve or think through his problem. . . . If he found a key person was in town and couldn't arrange lunch or dinner he would have breakfast with him. Usually after pleasantries or the lightness of a joke he would try to find out what was on this man's mind. Having done that, he would try to see if he couldn't suggest something that would be helpful to him. Sometimes he would bring problems back to the office and have a few of us dig up information and then he would write the fellow a letter. He just felt that he would like to be constructive and helpful. In doing this, the man would then begin to look to McKinsey as a person to whom he could bring a problem and get some help. This was both something I think Mac thoroughly enjoyed, but it was also something that was good for the firm. This was the combination.[7]

Clearly, McKinsey loved to analyze and exchange ideas. Newman commented that at one time McKinsey attended St. Louis University, attracted by its reputation for logic and analysis. Newman recalled that McKinsey liked to go back to St. Louis to see some of the priests who had been his teachers and argue the logic of their religious doctrine. "McKinsey had no particular religious interest himself. But he was intrigued with how one could reason from this proposition to that proposition."[8]

In a similar vein, McKinsey used conversation as a sales technique. Newman said:

McKinsey didn't pontificate. He was much more conversational. One of the standard techniques which he outlined to us in staff meetings was that you ask questions, you don't start giving answers. He often used an illustration about selling textbooks, emphasizing that first you learn what the teacher is concerned with and then explain how your book could help serve that purpose. He said, in the first place you can appear a lot smarter if you ask questions than you can if you simply give answers, but more than that—if you really try to help the other person—until you understand what the nature of his problem is, you had better not begin to guess how to go about it. He really was a super salesman . . . in the sense that he was a person that the other individuals liked. Having had a conversation with him or a dinner or a lunch, usually the other person went away somewhat stimulated and perhaps enriched. As I say, McKinsey did it morning, noon, and night.[9]

In attempting to understand McKinsey's style with clients and prospective clients, it is important to recognize that he enjoyed interviewing. One of his primary procedures for studying problems was to interview knowledgeable people. He emphasized this technique in training consultants, advising them to focus on the facts and to recognize that most people had reasons, such as boosting their egos or hiding problems, for distorting facts. Neukom described McKinsey's interviewing style:

Well, it was mostly a matter of sitting down in a comfortable setting and asking meaningful questions. He didn't take notes; he made mental notes of the answer rather than written notes. He was very informal. He would sit down with a chief executive and kick it around for a few hours. Sooner or later he got to the heart of the matter. He was just an old pro at this. The best kind of interviewing, of course, is the informal, where you have in mind something you want to achieve ultimately, but you do it in various ways. This is the kind of market research we did, too. We never did much quantitative research were you go out and punch doorbells. What we did was get hold of competent people in their field and then interview them in depth against a list of subjects: an interview guide. We would have about ten items on the agenda. . . . You often would start with number one. As the interview progressed you [might] jump to number eight and later come back to number six. By the time you got done you either exhausted the interviewee or exhausted the agenda.[10]

McKinsey had many ways of presenting himself favorably and was especially skilled in meeting with executive committees of clients. According to Goetz:

McKinsey told us that he often attended a meeting of the executive committee or the board of directors, and that his general tactic was to keep his mouth shut and listen to what went on. He found that usually everybody there had problems and wanted a chance to tell about them and how bad they were, and maybe get some sympathy or help.

And so when the sales manager was telling about his problems, nobody else was really listening much. The next man was getting his story ready mentally, and the finance man, when his turn came, also talked about his problems. When the meeting looked like it was about to close, McKinsey would speak up and say, "Gentlemen, it seems to me we have been talking about seven problems this afternoon. Now, problem number one is. . . . , and problem number two. . . . ," and he would name the seven problems.

Then he would say, "Now, problem number one breaks down into four sub-problems: one. . . , two. . . , three. . . , four. . . . Now sub-problem number one, we ought to know these things in order to answer that problem. Of these things, these we do know, and these we don't know, and either you should find out or you should hire me to find out."

And he would call the roll of all the major problems, and all the sub-problems, and all the factors and information needed to answer these things. He said he didn't restrict himself to the problems they had mentioned. It was easy to add any he wanted to because nobody would remember what anybody had said. And so, he would give a logical outline, first things first, the logical sequence in which things ought to be handled.

"When you reflect about it for a moment," Goetz commented, "this was a highly spectacular performance. He had the whole thing organized in the form of a study that ought to be made, the pieces that were missing, and how you would fit [them] together to get answers."[11]

With his consultants, McKinsey used to enjoy demonstrating the powers of a priori, analytical thinking. Goetz recalled, for example, how McKinsey advised one client just by analyzing the company's stationery carefully:

On one occasion he diagnosed the problems of a company from its letterhead. This was a manufacturer of air conditioners, a highly technical thing that requires salesmen to look at the customer's factory and measure the square feet of walls, doors, et cetera, and develop a whole installation. . . . Afterwards, it is a highly technical job to install it. This was a little company located in the Middle West. Its letterhead said, "Industrial Air Conditioning Installations − Coast to Coast from Canada to Mexico." McKinsey said, "You cannot sell these through manufacturing representatives, because they have to carry a number of lines to live on, and they [manufacturing representatives] can't be the kind of expert you want if they have to carry so many lines. So, you've got to have your own salesmen. Somebody on the West Coast wants a bid; six companies bid on it; your man has got to go out and make a survey in order to bid on it. Now, it takes three weeks to go over the bids with their [the client's] engineers to finally make a decision." Now, airplanes were pretty scarce at that time. McKinsey said, "What does your man do, take a train from Chicago, then three weeks later go out again if he's got the job? Or, does he stay out there to find out that one of the other five bidders got the job?"

He said that in any case, the travel expenses will eat up the profits. On the other hand, they [the client firm] should confine their activity to a radius of at most four or five hundred miles of Chicago. In fact, McKinsey was right: the company was doing badly.[12]

As he moved further into policy and actual adminstration, McKinsey tended to move from a quantitative approach to a qualitative one. Newman felt that McKinsey's greater exposure to day-to-day business activity led him to conclude that "many of the issues were subjective and intangible: and though he started in the quantitative area [in accounting], he moved out of that and didn't feel that the answers to the questions for most companies lay in getting more refined quantitative data."[13]

Newman traced McKinsey's development in this area back to the imposition of the income tax, which caused companies to improve their accounting. Given the existence of these figures, McKinsey sought to maximize their use to management, and this led to budgeting.

McKinsey soon found that if he was going to make a good budget that was really a plan of action, he wanted that budget related to responsibility. Traditional accounting usually computed cost of goods sold by starting with inventory, putting in labor and new materials and subtracting out what you have at the end of the year. But such accounts were not suitable to tie down the people. To relate financial results to executive responsibility, McKinsey urged a classification of accounts that matched company organization. But in many of his applications, the organization was fuzzy. This forced him into thinking about how you ought to organize for purposes of management. And once he got the organization, he still had a problem because he said if you are going to plan ahead and express expected results in terms of a budget, even though you have your organization, you need to know what's ahead and what your basic policies are. So he moved from budgets to organization and from organization to policy and outlook analysis. At the time I arrived, which would be ten years later than when this formulation had taken place, McKinsey had lost interest in budgeting per se; although all of the overall reports had a budget section, he had somebody else prepare the budget. He had gotten clearly over into seeing what the major problems of the business were, what policies were needed, and how you ought to organize to get this done. . . . [14]

Newman saw McKinsey as predominantly a clinician in the latter stages of his consulting career. "He wanted to use data but he didn't rely primarily on it."

In the analysis of the Marshall Field wholesale division, for example, McKinsey was concerned with future trends in distribution. It was a very thorough study of the outlook for general line dry goods wholesaling in the country. We spent quite a while getting supporting data but McKinsey knew what the answer was long before. . . .

He said, given the shift in transportation which permitted people to come into large shopping centers and the increasing interest in style, you had to have a way of moving merchandise to people which was speedier than you could get through the wholesaler. . . . Meanwhile, of course, he had studied a series of companies whose background supported this general analysis. He just knew the national wholesale dry goods firm was out of business. He didn't rely on hard data in that one study to demonstrate it in his own mind. He wanted enough data to convince others that he was sound. [15]

It appears, then, that McKinsey was endowed with a fabulous memory and great intuitive insights. In fact, every person interviewed who had worked with him cited dramatic examples of these characteristics. Newman said:

He soaked up information – this thing and that; weeks after visitng a company he would remember all sorts of things. Coupled with the memory was an uncanny capacity to organize and arrange data in some kind of a systematic fashion.

On several occasions when he was disgusted with a draft of a client report he got from his staff, he would say: "Well, come into the office and let me show you how to do it." He would sit us down and dictate for an hour and a half and never look at a note and have a completely logical sequence of topics. Yet he knew the major mission he was trying to convey; he knew his chief recommendations, and then would marshal the evidence to support each of these recommendations. There it was – a clear, integrated, factual report without reference to a written word or table.[16]

While it is true that McKinsey had superb mental faculties, it is also true that he worked hard at what he did. He was not a well-rounded man. He was interested in business management and how he could make it more effective; he was not interested in broader social issues except as they related to managing a business. The extent to which he put business above all is illustrated by his attitude toward his own and his employees' personal lives. Newman said that

One of the comments that McKinsey frequently made at staff meetings was that he knew that frequently we were asked to go off on engagements on short notice and that this undoubtedly caused a little problem at home. But he explained that he had made an understanding with his wife when she married him that she should recognize that she was making a choice of marrying a bookkeeper, which he assumed she didn't want to marry, or a man who was out to be successful. She should understand that being successful means that business comes first. We were supposed to take this story back and tell our wives. We never knew when, at 4:30 or 5:00 in the evening, we might be told, "Look, I just had a call and I want you to be in Detroit in the morning" and off we would go. We couldn't make a social engagement without telling the hostess that we expected to be able to go, but our business was such that we often got emergency calls. As far as McKinsey was concerned, he had no compunction about breaking into any sort of commitments we had. That was the way in which he lived and he expected us to live that way too.[17]

Although McKinsey was in his own way a genius, research for this book substantiates the comment made by Thomas Alva Edison: "Genius is one per cent inspiration and ninety-nine per cent perspiration." For example, McKinsey was known for his memory for humorous stories. In talking to his colleagues, it appeared that he just soaked them up for instantaneous recall. Actually, he worked at building his repertoire. His nephew Walter McKinsey recalled asking McKinsey how he remembered all those stories:

He said, "Well, what you do is write them down and write enough of them so that you remember them. Because in 10 years most people will have forgotten them. . . . All you have to do is bring them up to date. You will find you can adopt any story to any situation you happen to want." He had his black book in which he kept a great many of his very wonderful stories. [18]

His feats of memory in analyzing firms were also aided by hard work. Over the years he developed a mental set for viewing a firm. As a result, he approached each business setting with a framework and reference point for gathering and interpreting data. Although at first he was not conscious of that framework, he eventually became aware of it and put it into writing. Its intellectual heritage is readily traceable to his work in budgeting, finance, managerial accounting, and business policy.

Newman recalled that McKinsey's framework came to be put into writing because he was having trouble giving the staff a way of thinking. Newman remembers Tom Kearney urging him, "When you say 'way of thinking' you mean that there is a certain arrangement of topics: a certain sequence in which you look at the company, the way you deal with it. Why don't you put this down on paper so that the people will understand it?" At first McKinsey was reluctant to put an outline on paper for fear that his staff would follow it slavishly, rather than using only those parts that were relevant to the problem at hand. But Kearney finally prevailed, and staff members were given a six-page typed document called "A General Survey Outline." [19] This outline became the bible of McKinsey consultants. Goetz says that the outline helped a McKinsey consultant look good from the time he entered the door:

If you followed [McKinsey's] outline, you would begin asking pertinent questions that indicated you had a deep perception of business. You would begin on sales policies: What are your product lines? In this product, what are the sizes, styles, colors, and so on. . . . What classes of customers do you sell to? What are your sales appeals, . . . pricing policies, et cetera?

By going through the entire outline in this way, the consultant was provided an organized approach to a study, continuity in asking questions, and a framework within which the client's critical information could be remembered. Goetz

recalls that the outline had other advantages: "You let the client talk. And you simply fitted his answers into the outline. Whenever he stopped, you asked the first question he hadn't answered. That would start him talking again, and you skipped any questions that he already answered. You didn't have to take notes, because you had the outline. When you left, you could go over the outline, and the questions would remind you of what answers he had given."[20]

In summary, as a consultant, McKinsey worked hard at ordering his thinking, attracting clients, and getting a reputation for being one of the best in the field. His general survey outline provides the major insights into his approach to consulting. Because of this, we will look at it in detail in the next chapter.

One other aspect of McKinsey's philosophy should be emphasized. According to Bower, "He was always sensitive to people's feelings and attitudes, and as a consultant recognized that rational thinking does not necessarily control decisions or actions."[21] Thus, although McKinsey sought facts, he knew that facts alone were not enough. The successful manager needs good intuition, hunch, and judgment, as well as facts.

Notes

1.   The history of these firms goes back to 1935, when McKinsey became chairman of the board of Marshall Field and Company. According to Marvin Bower (correspondence, August 31, 1977):

When McKinsey's chairmanship was announced, he received about a dozen letters from firms that wanted to acquire James O. McKinsey and Company. Among these was one from C. Oliver Wellington of Scovell, Wellington & Company, an accounting and consulting firm of some prestige. McKinsey and Wellington got together one weekend at McKinsey's home and worked out the establishment of McKinsey, Wellington & Company to carry on the consulting practice of both firms; and the consulting partners and associates joined that firm. The small accounting practice of James O. McKinsey and Company was transferred to Scovell, Wellington & Company. Finally, McKinsey, Wellington and Scovell, Wellington had four common partners.

Following McKinsey's death, the affiliation with Scovell, Wellington & Company was discontinued; and two separate consulting firms, affiliated by contract, were established: McKinsey & Company, with offices in New York and Boston, and McKinsey, Kearney & Company of Chicago. Some years later, this affiliation was terminated; and McKinsey, Kearney & Company changed its name to A. T. Kearney & Company, because McKinsey & Company wanted to become a national firm and have its own office in Chicago.

2.   Neukom, *McKinsey Memoirs*, p. 3.

3.   Ibid., p. 27.

4.   Interview, August 15, 1972.

5.   Interview, October 3, 1975.

6. Interview, July 1, 1976.

7. Interview, February 16, 1973.

8. Ibid.

9. Ibid.

10. Neukom, *McKinsey Memoirs,* p. 16.

11. Interview, August 15, 1972.

12. Ibid. In commenting about this case, Bower recalled that McKinsey backed up his deductions with a thorough analysis before he advised the client.

13. Interview, February 16, 1973.

14. Ibid.

15. Ibid.

16. Ibid.

17. Ibid.

18. Interview, July 1, 1976.

19. Interview, February 16, 1973.

20. Interview, August 15, 1972.

21. Correspondence, September 1, 1977.

Chapter IV

The Diagnostic Approach

McKinsey's diagnostic approach to business firms is one of his greatest contributions to management. It was the essential foundation of McKinsey's strategy in training junior consultants, and it provided the basic structure for one of the most widely used business policy texts, *Business Policies and Management*. [1]

To appreciate McKinsey's approach, it is essential to go back to his conception of a business organization as an open system that needs to be viewed holistically. In his consulting he focused on the diagnosis of the organization as a whole and the relation of the totality to the firm's major policies. He was interested in general management rather than the specialized fields and functional areas such as marketing and industrial engineering. In his consulting, he constantly emphasized the need to center activities on issues dealing with the major policies of the firm and the strategies needed to implement them. Although McKinsey's firm did have specialists in the functional areas of management and contracted for special studies, McKinsey preferred to approach clients' firms from the point of view of top management.

Marvin Bower, managing director of McKinsey and Company for many years, was in a good position to identify the elements of McKinsey's approach and to evaluate them as they were put into practice. He believes that "McKinsey's greatest contribution to consulting as well as to business was his concept of the integrated nature of managing a business." This concept, as we have seen, views the processes of management as interacting. According to Bower, this basic concept came from McKinsey's thinking about budgeting as it is reflected in *Budgetary Control*.

That was the emphasis that he put into our consulting work. He didn't just take a look at something without putting it in perspective and trying to evaluate it in the framework of the total enterprise and relating it to profits.

Mac's second contribution to consulting was his demonstration of independence by thought and deed — his willingness to tell the client the truth as he saw it. This is a foundation stone of the professional approach, although Mac never talked about professionalism even though he practiced it. And despite his being a teacher, he did not try to codify or teach professionalism as such — that came along later.

Another contribution of Mac's to consulting was the general survey approach, that is, the making of a diagnosis of problems based on an overall examination of the business. That was called for in the thirties when so many companies were operating unprofitably and the causes and corrections had to be determined. [2]

The General Survey Outline

The logical outcome of McKinsey's approach was a procedure in which the consultant seeks the facts, puts them into perspective, and, in so doing, brings the central problems into focus. McKinsey wrote the General Survey Outline as an aid in gathering the relevant facts. The outline is a guide for analyzing a business. It brings into focus most of the information needed and provides a framework for arranging it revealingly.

Before reading the General Survey Outline, it is good to remember that McKinsey resisted writing it. He was afraid that it would be misinterpreted and misused. He wanted it to be a guide to thinking. His concern was that it would be used in a rote manner to substitute for thinking. To McKinsey, rigorous analytical thinking was the key to successful consulting. Walter McKinsey recalled that "McKinsey frequently commented that most people, being lazy, didn't like to think. They never thought through a whole problem . . . because they never approached it in the right manner."[3]

The outline is thus a guide to rigorous thinking in the form of a basic framework derived from McKinsey's general theory of management. Successful McKinsey consultants committed it to memory and used it to ask the right questions, integrate the facts, and make a diagnosis. In short, the outline provided a perspective and philosophy for consulting in the McKinsey manner. Neukom commented that "although various members of the firm had undertaken over the years to revise and strengthen it, the last [1962] edition to appear in [the firm's] training manual is surprisingly similar to the original version I was given when I joined the firm in 1934."[4]

The underlying strategy of McKinsey's outline requires the consultant to:

1. Understand the general nature of the business. A review of its history for at least the last ten years provides a perspective on the total enterprise in terms of company strategy and the forces impinging upon it.

2. Evaluate the general environment in which the company operates. This starts with the broader economic and political setting and narrows to an outlook for the industry and the company's position in the industry.

3. Evaluate the company in three broad areas: the organization structure, technology, facilities, and staffing; policies in the functional areas of management such as sales, production, purchasing, finances, and personnel; and finances and financial requirements. The facts gathered in this broad and detailed analysis should enable the consultant to determine the current problems facing a company, to explain those problems, and to suggest some solutions.

What follows is a complete copy of the General Survey Outline as it was rewritten for the training program of McKinsey, Wellington and Company around 1936. This revised edition was supplied by John Neukom, and is an expanded version of the first edition. Although McKinsey would probably have balked at such a lengthy and elaborate revision, it is presented here because it gives the reader a clearer insight into the McKinsey approach than does the rather skeletal outline found in the first edition.

The General Survey Outline
(Revised Edition, circa 1936)

MAJOR TOPICS TO BE COVERED
The major topics to be covered in a complete general survey are the following:

I. Cause and nature of present problems
II. Outlook for company
III. Policies
IV. Administrative organization
V. Executive personnel
VI. Facilities
VII. Controls and procedures
VIII. Financial condition
IX. Financial requirements

In a complete general survey these topics become report section headings. Conclusions and recommendations shall be treated as discussed under "Context" in the manual of report standards. There may be exceptions to the use of these topics as report section heads. In an unusually comprehensive survey topics subordinate to the foregoing may become section heads. The "Outlook for Company," for example, may be presented in two report sections, "Outlook for Industry" and "Position of Company in Industry"; policies may be divided into several report sections, "Sales Policies," "Production Policies," and so on.

On the other hand, in a less detailed study certain combinations of the foregoing topics may be presented in a single section. Examples of combination are: "Organization" and "Personnel," (4) and (5), in one section, "Organization and Personnel"; and "Financial Condition" and "Financial Requirements," (8) and (9), into "Financial Condition and Requirements."

In Class III and IV reports, topics which are subordinate to breakdowns of the foregoing topics may become section headings. In a study of sales policies (one phase of the breakdown of "Policies"), for example, "Products," "Types of Customers," and so on, may become section headings. Standardization in this regard is impossible.

The remainder of this memorandum shall be devoted to consideration of each of the major topics listed heretofore in (1) through (9).

I. CAUSE AND NATURE OF PRESENT PROBLEMS

Factors to be considered
Study of the nature of and reasons for a client's problems necessitates consideration of the following:

1. *History of the Company.* In report presentation the "History of the Company" should be in chronological outline form with emphasis on the developments which have contributed to present problems of the company. In the event of financial problems, financial condition should be summarized. In cases where the client's problem can be traced to industry developments, a brief chronological resume of pertinent events in industry history should be included.

2. *Causes of Present Problems.* In report presentation summarize the "Causes of Present Problems" of the company. These reasons will usually arise from one or more of the following:

    a. Business conditions
    b. Conditions of the industry
    c. Unsound policies or organization
    d. Inadequate facilities or procedures
    e. Ineffective executive personnel

In some cases, the reasons for present problems are apparent from the discussion in (1), and it may not be necessary to include this topic.

3. *Present Problems of Company.* In report presentation summarize the "Present Problems of Company."

4. *Method of Investigation.* In report presentation list the significant steps taken in conducting the investigation and indicate the scope of each. Steps should be listed clearly and comprehensively to indicate to the client the extent of our work. This section should end with a list of the subsequent sections in the report provided report sections are not listed in the letter of transmittal.

In preparing this section of the report the material should be presented under sideheads as underlined above. In cases where it may be more clear to use additional sideheads the report writer may do so, provided the flow from sidehead to sidehead is logical.

As stated in the Manual of Report Standards, the section "Cause and Nature of Present Problems" should not be included in Financing Survey Reports. To quote from the manual: "Consequently the content of the first section should be confined to a description of the company's history and operations...."

II. OUTLOOK FOR COMPANY

Objective

The objective of this section is the determination of the long-term profit possibilities of the company. In this connection we should consider:

1. Outlook for the industry in which the company operates
2. Position of the company in that industry

Outlook for industry

Outlook for the profitability of the industry in which the company is engaged will require a consideration of the following:

1. The *volume* of sales which can be procured. This determination should be based upon an appraisal of the actual or potential demand for the industry's products in terms of consumer, customer industries, and so on. This, in turn, requires an appraisal of the factors affecting the demand of consumers, each customer industry, and so on.

For example, in determining the volume outlook for the malting industry it is necessary to determine the important customer groups, which in this case are the brewing and distilling industries. Then it is necessary to determine the effect of such factors as general business conditions, drinking habits, production methods, and so on, on the demand of these industries for malt.

Where raw material industries are involved, the supply factor may become important in connection with the volume consideration. When the consumer market is considered, final conclusions as to the actual and potential market should be developed.

2. The *prices* at which the volume indicated in (1) can be sold. This determination should be based upon all of the factors affecting price, such factors as competitive conditions, general business conditions, legislation and the like.

3. The *cost* of the volume indicated in (1) sold at the prices indicated in (2). This necessitates considering the factors which affect the following cost classifications: Production costs (material, labor, and overhead), selling costs, administrative costs, taxation, and so on.

Consideration of the foregoing will result in the following formula: (Volume x (price − cost) = profit. This is the objective of this sub-section.

In a report, presentation of the discussion of each of the foregoing usually should commence with a statement showing the historical background of each factor. This material should be submitted under sideheads as underlined in the foregoing, together with such minor sideheads as are necessary. Organization of the material in complicated studies may necessarily vary from that indicated. Variance in such cases is permissible, provided the profit concept of the outlook is not sacrificed.

Position of company

The position of a given company in its industry can be determined by analysis of its:

1. *Statistical Position.* This can be ascertained by comparison of its sales and profit experience (and other significant factors) with that of the industry and major competitors.

2. *Reputation with the Trade.* This can generally be determined by means of analysis of complaints, discussions with informed individuals, and field survey.

3. Other significant factors such as: Plant location, production soundness, type of outlets, and so on. In the case of financially distressed companies, the attitude of creditors to any reorganization may be a very significant consideration.

In report presentation material relating to company position should be discussed under sideheadings as indicated in (1) and (2), and other appropriate sideheadings in the case of factors in (3).

Determination of the foregoing should show the present position of the company. Its future position and consequent profitability will generally be dependent upon the effectiveness of management. At this point we should indicate that our appraisal of the effectiveness of management is discussed throughout the remainder of the report.

This section of the report should conclude with a summary of the favorable and unfavorable factors which may affect the future of the company, and conclusions. Caution in presenting conclusions must obviously be exercised. Always avoid the positive where doubt exists, and do not hesitate to include legitimate hedges.

III. POLICIES

Policies to be considered

A careful study should be made of the policies of the client company with reference to the following groups of activities:

1. Sales
2. Production
3. Purchasing
4. Financial
5. Personnel

Policies relating to each of these activities are interrelated to a considerable degree.

A. Sales policies

In this connection the investigator should consider policies relating to:

1. Products
2. Customers
3. Channels of distribution
4. Pricing
5. Sales appeals
6. Sales promotion
7. Sales direction and supervision

In report presentation, headings relating to these policies should be in these words and in this sequence. In particular cases, it may be desirable to make combinations of these topics into a single heading; "Sales Appeals" and "Sales Promotion," for example, can be presented as "Sales Appeals and Promotion." If no problems exist with reference to any of these policies, obviously the particular sub-section should not be included in the report.

PRODUCTS
The purpose of this study is to determine if the client's policies governing products are such as to provide for the offering of the number and kinds of products which are best adapted to the market. Study of product policies will involve consideration of:

1. Number and variety
2. Design and style
3. Quality

Number and Variety
In considering this topic determine:

1. The total number of items sold by the company and the relative importance of the sales of each.

2. The major groups into which they can be classified and the relative importance of the sales of each.

3. On the basis of (1) and (2), desirable additions to or eliminations from the line. This involves consideration of:
    a. Whether it is sound and economical to have all of these items or groups sold by one company. Consider also the effect on company reputation.

    b. Whether other items or groups of items are desirable in order to supplement the line and provide proper diversification to better meet the demands of customers, level seasonal and cyclical fluctuations in operations, and replace volume lost through long term individual product or product group sales declines.

    c. Whether the variety in each group is satisfactory in view of customer demands and manufacturing, selling and overhead costs.

    d. Whether additional products will protect the customer relationships of the company from competitor invasion.

e. Whether a change in products should be made in view of the nature of the company's management, sales organization, production organization, facilities and financial strength.

Once possible new products have been suggested in line with the above requirements, a procedure should be established for testing the suitability of these products. In this connection it is generally advisable to:

1. Carefully select test markets where it will be possible to conveniently secure an unbiased reaction to these products.

2. Design the test campaign so that it will indicate the most effective policies regarding customers, channels of distribution, pricing, appeals and promotion.

Design and Style
In considering this topic, study the trend in and nature of the demand with reference to:

1. Use
2. Size
3. Pattern, color, and other style factors

The significance of each of these factors depends upon the nature of the product and whether it is intended for industrial or consumer use.

Sales volume may frequently be increased through more radical styling or creating or shortening the style cycle, thereby creating style obsolescence at relatively frequent intervals. On the other hand, these changes may have costly effects upon manufacturing costs and inventory. If client styling is inadequate, the investigator should weigh the relative desirability of training present styling personnel, securing new stylists, or retaining professional style counsel.

Quality
For considering quality it is necessary to determine the standing of the company's products from the point of view of:

1. Experts in the field
2. The trade, as determined by analysis of complaints in the field survey

Generally the company's quality standing should correspond with that generally accepted by the trade as necessary for the market the company attempts to serve. Any shortcomings in this regard must be noted. Slightly higher standards than the industry average may be desirable. If the company's standards greatly exceed those of competitors, the company is probably incurring increased costs and should reduce quality to protect profit margins and insure competitive prices.

CUSTOMERS
The purpose of this study is to determine if the client's policies governing customers provide for selling those customers which can be served most profitably. Study of customer policies will involve a consideration of:

1. Type of customers
2. Size and number of customers
3. Geographical location of customers

"Customers" can be defined as the accounts to which the company actually sells. Therefore jobbers or retailers or consumers can be "Customers," depending upon the channels of distribution of the client. In cases where the client sells to other than consumers, the influence, if important, of consumer groups should generally be presented in reports in the "Outlook for the Company." In cases where the client sells to wholesalers, who in turn sell to retailers, the influence of retailer groups should logically be presented in the "Customer" section in connection with the appraisal of the wholesaler customers. It obviously may be necessary in the "Customer" section to refer to or repeat conclusions regarding consumers as stated in the Outlook section.

Type
The client customer policy must be analyzed to determine whether the types of customers sold are such as to permit the effective cultivation of the potential market defined in the "Outlook for the Company" section. This analysis should be pointed up to indicate whether:

1. Profitable types of customers have been overlooked
2. Types of customers are cultivated whose characteristics make them unprofitable

In this connection it is also important to determine whether the client attempts to serve customers whose needs would supply volume for idle plant capacity. For example, a machinery manufacturer may find it wise to do some "job" work in the foundry.

Size and Number
The client sales experience should be analyzed on the basis of sales brackets (volume ranges) to determine the number of customers in each bracket and the proportion of total sales accounted for by each bracket. This analysis should indicate whether:

1. The client has concentrated its sales among too few customers.
2. A large number of very small and probably unprofitable accounts are being served.
3. The company is spreading its selling efforts unwisely by serving too many accounts.

If the customer problem is an important one, it may be desirable to make a detailed cost study in connection with the determination of what constitutes an unprofitable account. Obviously, the effect of reduced volume on manufacturing costs, the ability of salesmen to earn a living, and so on, must be given consideration in cases where the elimination of certain accounts may be deemed advisable.

Geographical Location
The location of client sales volume should be analyzed to determine:

1. The extent to which the company is reaching the potential market ascertained in the "Outlook for the Company."

2. Whether unprofitable territories are cultivated, unprofitable either because of inadequate potential or uneconomical location (with respect to shipping and selling expense).

CHANNELS OF DISTRIBUTION
Study of channels of distribution is directed at the determination of the most economical method of reaching the customers which the company should seek to sell as determined in the preceding sections. This analysis involves consideration of the following:

1. *Present channels of distribution* (of client). In studying this question, the investigator should ascertain the following:
- **a.** The volume of sales through each channel of distribution now utilized by the company
- **b.** The percentage of the potential sales through each channel which the company is receiving
- **c.** The changes the company has made in its methods of distribution and the results of these changes

2. *Effectiveness of present channels.* In determining this, give consideration to:
- **a.** Nature of product line
- **b.** Type, size, number and location of the customers the client should serve
- **c.** Requirements of the customers as regards delivery, size and frequency of order, and so on
- **d.** Pricing and sales promotion requirements
- **e.** Sales volume which client is seeking
- **f.** Competitive practices

3. *Recommendations regarding channels.* In making recommendations consider available channels of distribution and select those best suited:
- **a.** To meet requirements considered in (2)
- **b.** By their nature, considering availability, cost, competition within each channel and the like

PRICING
The objective of this study is to ascertain if the client offers his products at prices which provide the most satisfactory profit. This can be achieved by first determining the theoretical price, which is actual cost plus a reasonable profit. This theoretical price should then be adjusted to recognize:

1. Industry practice
2. Competitive conditions
3. Economic conditions
4. Price legislation
5. Special conditions relating to specific transactions

Theoretical Price
In determining actual cost, the first step in establishing theoretical prices, the investigator should give consideration to all the elements which enter into costs, such as:

- **a.** Raw materials
- **b.** Direct labor
- **c.** Indirect manufacturing expenses
- **d.** Administrative expenses
- **e.** Freight cost

f.   Selling expenses, including discounts, advertising expenditures, and so on

The investigator should seek to determine if the policy of the company in determining each of these expenses and in controlling their amount is correct. He should give particular attention to the effect of excess capacity and the cost of capital on the production cost of products. He should determine if a revaluation of assets or the elimination of the carrying charges on unused production capacity would materially affect the cost of manufacturing. He should also carefully consider whether the policy of the company with reference to freight charges, discounts and terms of credit is proper. In short, he should seek to determine the actual cost of the products offered for sale.

The theoretical price is obtained by adding a reasonable profit to the actual cost. In determining what constitutes a reasonable profit the investigator should give consideration to:

a.   The going rate of return on the capital invested
b.   The degree of risk involved in the particular industry

Industry Practice

It must be recognized that client pricing policies should be in line with those generally accepted by the industry, provided industry pricing practice is sound. Many industries have common practices such as basing point systems, discount schedules, freight allowances, and so on.

Competitive Conditions

The investigator should seek to ascertain the prices of competitors for products comparable to those of the client and determine whether the client is losing its market because it is being undersold. If so, he should ascertain whether it would be beneficial to the client from the long run point of view to meet competitive conditions at the present. He should also ascertain the extent to which there is cooperation with competitors on price problems. Experience has shown that in most lines of industry, it is not feasible for competitors to attempt to stabilize prices for the industry as a whole. It is desirable for competitors to agree with reference to general policies and for local representatives of competitors to seek to prevent a demoralization of the market by cut-throat competitive methods.

Economic Conditions

The investigator should give careful consideration to economic conditions and the possible trend of these conditions in determining what the pricing policy of the client should be. It is obvious that in a period of declining prices, the client must adjust its prices quickly to maintain its position in the market. The ability of a company to judge when and to what degree prices should be adjusted is an important test of the ability of its management. To make such adjustment wisely requires adequate information and good judgment. Careful consideration should also be given to the type of customers to whom the client desires to appeal and the effect of price adjustments on the attitude of these customers toward the client. For example, a retail specialty store appealing to a selected clientele may injure its prestige by offering low price merchandise as a means of seeking a larger number of customers. This aspect of pricing is exceedingly important and the investigator has an opportunity to render constructive service by aiding the management to determine the price which will secure the volume which will yield the largest returns.

Price Legislation
The investigator should be certain that the client's pricing policies and practices do not violate national and local legislation. The provisions of the Robinson-Patman Act and other current and prospective legislation make this an important consideration.

Special Conditions
The investigator should recognize that special conditions may affect the application of a client's pricing policies in individual transactions. For example, it may be advisable to price on the basis of "differential costs" in certain cases. In other cases it may be wise to make concessions for "sales promotion" reasons. The client pricing policies should be sufficiently flexible to meet these and similar situations.

In studying this problem, the future of the client as well as his immediate needs must be given careful consideration. There is probably no more important question of policy than determining the price which will yield the volume which will produce the cost which will result in the largest net return from a long run point of view. An answer to this question involves a consideration of most of the major questions of policy which we shall discuss in this outline.

SALES APPEAL
The objective of this study is to determine the basis on which the client should appeal to his customers to purchase his products. The appeals which are inherent to either the product or client organization are the following:

1. Quality
2. Price
3. Style and design
4. Package
5. Service
6. Reputation of company
7. Personality and ability of salesmen
8. Reciprocity

Products may also be promoted on the basis of appeals which are not inherent to either product or organization. For example, a box of chocolates may be promoted as an aid to romance.

In determining the most desirable sales appeals the investigator should determine, for each type of customer:

1. Who makes the decision (consumer, salesperson, retailer, and so on) regarding the purchase of the product.

2. The appeals which influence this decision. Obviously, in the case of most products, the decision to buy may be made partly by one individual and partly by another. In such cases, the investigator must be sure to determine the appeals which influence the contribution to the final decison made by each. If possible, he should determine this attitude by personal contact with representative customers of each type. In case it is not possible to conduct a field study, it will then be necessary for the investigator to consider each of these appeals in terms of his previous experience and the experience of the company as

determined from the opinions of executives and the results shown by its records.

SALES PROMOTION

The purpose of this study is to determine the best methods to promote the appeals which influence the purchase of the product. In this connection it is necessary to consider sales promotional activities of the following types:

1. Advertising
2. Personal solicitation

Advertising

Advertising from the point of view of our studies includes all means of reaching the customer other than by the personal contact of representatives of the company. The major purposes of advertising are the following:

1. To bring customers to a selling place where they can be sold by merchandise displays, salesperson efforts, and so on
2. To persuade the customer to ask for a specific product
3. To produce direct sales
4. To assist the salesperson in making sales when he approaches the customer
5. To build institutional good will

Any company, obviously, may use advertising for one or more of these reasons.

In studying this problem, the investigator should determine the following:

1. The extent to which advertising can be used effectively to present each of the desirable appeals so as to accomplish any of the foregoing objectives.

2. The type (institutional, reader, display, testimonial, and so on) and amount of advertising which can be used most effectively for this purpose. This may necessitate the preparation of an advertising budget.

3. The mediums (radio, newspaper, magazine, billboard, point of sale, trade papers, direct mail, display, and so on) through which this advertising can be presented most effectively.

It is desirable that the investigator secure information by contacts in the field whenever possible. It should be realized that in most cases it is not possible to make long term final decisions regarding (2) and (3) during any study. The investigator, therefore, should establish techniques which permit the continuous measurement of the relative effectiveness of all advertising effort.

Personal Solicitation

In studying this problem, the investigator should determine the following:

1. The extent to which personal solicitation can be used to present each of the desirable sales appeals.

2. The nature of the activity which must be carried on to make this personal solicitation effective.

3. The extent to which this activity should be carried by any or all of the following:
   a. Direct sales representatives
   b. Missionary or service men
   c. Executives

4. The requisite qualifications of the individual in (3) to carry on the activities in (2). This may involve a consideration of the policy of the company with reference to the selection, training and compensation of its sales personnel, which should be discussed under "Personnel Policies."

5. The techniques best adapted to carrying on the activities in (2).

SALES DIRECTION AND SUPERVISION
The purpose of this study is to determine the nature and extent of the direction and supervision of sales activities that the client should exercise and the techniques for securing proper direction and supervision. Consequently the investigator should ascertain:

1. The activities which are to be supervised such as:
   a. Salesman calls
   b. Product emphasis
   c. Customer activities
   d. Promotional campaigns
   e. And so on

2. Whether the techniques used by the company give adequate control of these activities.

3. What additional techniques should be employed:
   a. Sales and conferences
   b. Sales reports
   c. Field trips
   d. Sales contests
   e. And so on

Material for this study can be secured most effectively by traveling in the field with certain client sales representatives. This method permits the investigator to observe the salesman at work and to discuss pertinent questions with him between calls. When traveling with a salesman it is often most effective for the investigator to be introduced to the trade as a "trainee" of the client's sales organization.

B. Production policies

TOPICS TO BE CONSIDERED
Study of production policies involves a study of policies relating to:

1. Products to produce
2. Manufacturing processes
3. Production planning
4. Production standards
5. Operating control

PRODUCTS TO PRODUCE
The investigator should appraise client policies regarding product manufacture with regard to:

1. Product design. This necessitates consideration of:
   a. Market requirements
   b. Economy of production: Standardization of piece parts, and so on
   c. Quality requirements

2. Desirability of manufacturing or purchasing finished products, piece parts or subassemblies or materials. This involves consideration of:
   a. Relative economy. This may involve securing competitive bids from probable suppliers. In making comparisons consideration must be given to any idle plant costs which might result.
   b. Ability of management
   c. Reliability of supply (availability of proper quantities at desired time)
   d. Permanence and stability of demand for product

Consideration of the foregoing may necessitate the disposition or acquisition of facilities. In report presentation this should be discussed with "Facilities."

MANUFACTURING PROCESSES
Determination of proper processes involves consideration of:

1. The various commercial processes available for manufacturing the product in accordance with specified quality standards
2. Relative economy of these processes
3. Effect of future product demand on choice of processes

PRODUCTION PLANNING
The investigator should determine whether in planning production the client has given sufficient consideration to:

1. Coordination of sales and production, taking into account seasonal fluctuations and other special conditions
2. Economical lot size, from the manufacturing viewpoint
3. Most economical sequence of operations, to meet quality standards. In this connection it may be necessary to consider layout. In report presentation, this discussion should be presented under "Facilities."
4. Economical storage and handling requirements

PRODUCTION STANDARDS
The investigator should determine:

1. Whether means for determining and applying standard manufacturing methods is sound
2. Whether standard practice instructions have been set up covering these methods
3. Whether adequate means of enforcing these standards have been established

OPERATING CONTROLS
The manufacturing controls which should be considered are:

1. Production control
2. Inventory control
3. Quality control

Production Control
The investigator should appraise client policies with regard to:

1. Authorization of production
2. Routing
3. Scheduling
4. Dispatching
5. Follow up

The significant objectives of production control are customer service and minimum production costs.

Inventory Control
The investigator should appraise client policies with regard to the following relating to manufacturing inventories:

1. Determination of material requirements
2. Transmitting these requirements to purchasing department
3. Storing an adequate supply
4. Issuing and delivering stores as wanted

The significant objectives of inventory control are:

1. Provision of adequate stocks to permit requisite service to customers
2. Permission to manufacture in economical lot sizes
3. Leveling of production peaks and valleys
4. Maintenance of minimum inventories compatible with (1), (2) and (3)

Quality Control
The investigator should appraise client policies with regard to:

1. Physical or chemical testing of raw materials, materials in process, or finished goods
2. Operating or field tests of finished goods
3. Inspection of the finished product

The significant objectives of quality control are the determination of the fitness of the product for sale, or where grading is involved, the grade under which the product is to be sold.

Whenever it is necessary to discuss in detail any of the procedures relating to the above controls, that discussion should be presented in the section on Controls and Procedures as provided therein.

Further breakdown of the majority of these topics is contained in the training manual in the outline for an investigation of manufacturing activities.

C. Purchasing policies

TOPICS TO BE CONSIDERED
The study of purchasing policies involves consideration of:

1. Size of purchase
2. Quality standards
3. Price determination
4. Selection of vendors
5. Control of inventories

It is important to consider purchasing policies broadly, not just those followed by the centralized purchasing department. In a department store, or mail order company, for example, each buyer may have established different purchasing policies.

In report presentation, material should be discussed under these sideheadings, unless circumstances justify the elimination of a heading, or greater breakdown, in which case factors and considerations listed herein as (1), (2) and so on might be elevated to a minor or major sidehead position.

SIZE OF PURCHASE
Determination of the size of purchase to be made (and an appraisal of client policy in this regard) necessitates consideration of:

1. The minimum and maximum economical purchase size. The major factors which must be considered in this determination are:
   a. Requirements of the client operating (sales, production and so on depending upon the items in question) program. This may involve study of the client sales outlook, production period, and so on.
   b. Economical shipping quantities
   c. Economical handling quantities
   d. Economical price quantitites (quantity discounts, etc.)
   e. Possibility of obsolescence or deterioration
   f. Storage capacity
2. The time at which purchases should be made. This involves study of:
   a. Availability of the desired items. If available only at certain times, obviously size of purchase is affected.
   b. Time required by suppliers to make delivery.
   c. Desirability of purchasing in advance of requirements. This involves study of price trends, and so on. Under certain conditions, such as supplier price advance notices, this may be desirable. Consistent speculation on price, however, should be avoided.
   d. Industry Practice.

QUALITY STANDARDS
The major considerations in this regard are the following:

1. Whether quality standards and written specifications have been established. Consider possible economies through standardization. (This may affect other than quality.)
2. Whether these quality standards are satisfactory to:
   a. Meet market requirements, or the requirements of the requisitioning department
   b. Assure maximum economy. In other words, can quality standards be lowered without affecting operations adversely?

3. Whether inspection of incoming goods is adequate to assure the meeting of quality (and other) specifications

PRICE DETERMINATION
This is an important consideration, and involves study of:

1. The method by which the client determines the prices he can afford to pay. This is of obvious significance from a profit viewpoint, especially in the purchase of raw materials or piece parts to be used in products the resale price of which is determined by competitive levels. This study may necessitate analysis of pricing policies or market conditions, or both.

2. Within the limits established in (1), the manner in which prices that must be paid are determined. Consider the extent to which the purchaser utilizes competitive bidding. In many companies, competitive bidding and a permanent record of all bids are required.

In report presentation, avoid under this sidehead the unnecessary discussion of material relating to prices paid which has been discussed under other sideheads under "Purchasing Policies."

SELECTION OF VENDORS
This involves consideration of:

1. The advantages and disadvantages of buying from one or several vendors. In this connection consider:
   a. Continuous assurance of source
   b. Service
   c. Advantages of competitive bidding
   d. And so on

2. Specific source selection. Consider whether purchaser has given adequate consideration to quality, price, service, and so on in selecting specific sources. In certain cases this may justify contacting suppliers of similar merchandise. Be alert to detect "rake off" or "friendship" purchasing; on the other hand, constantly bear in mind the possibilities of selecting sources so as to capitalize reciprocal possibilities.

CONTROL OF INVENTORIES
This involves a consideration of the extent to which the activities of the purchasing and operating departments are coordinated with financial requirements. Consider:

1. The use of minimums and maximums. In this connection, consider inventory balance.

2. Excess or obsolete inventory liquidation, from the timing, pricing and overall profit viewpoint. In this connection, determine whether inventories are such as to assure the minimum (possible) charges with regard to:
   a. Interest on investment
   b. Insurance
   c. Property taxes
   d. Space charges (light, heat, building charges or rent)
   e. Handling costs

D. Personnel policies

TOPICS TO BE CONSIDERED
The study of personnel policies involves a consideration of:

1. Selection
2. Training
3. Compensation
4. Employee benefits
5. Discharge
6. Public and industrial relations

SELECTION

Selection of personnel should be based upon policies governing:

1. Sources. Personnel may be secured from:
   a. Within the company. Securing personnel for particular positions through advancement within the company is frequently desirable because they are familiar with company operations; it is easier to appraise the candidates on their record; and employee morale is affected favorably. When promotions occur within the company it is wise to consider the desirability of horizontal vs. vertical promotion and securing assistants who complement rather than supplement superiors.
   b. Without the company. It is often preferable to secure necessary personnel for particular work from without the company: When specialized training or ability of a sort not available in the company is required; when unexpected vacancies occur before candidates within the company have been properly prepared; and when a new point of view seems desirable.

2. Standards of selection. The investigator should determine whether the client has undertaken an analysis of the jobs in the company to determine their requirements, and whether these have been set forth in writing in the form of standards to be used as the basis for selecting employees for specific jobs. Candidates' ability to meet the requirements developed above should generally be determined on the basis of:
   a. Experience
   b. Education, both technical and general
   c. Geographical background
   d. Religion to prevent cliques and prejudices
   e. Relationship to present employees to limit "family" groups
   f. Sex

The investigator should also appraise client methods and procedures involved in personnel selection.

Standards and techniques for appraising executive personnel are considered in Section VI — Executive Personnel in this outline.

TRAINING

In appraising a training program or determining the need for one it is necessary to consider:

1. The extent of the need for training. This is dependent upon the nature of the client business (by types of activity within the business) and the type and capabilities of personnel the client can secure.

2. The type of training program best fitted to satisfy the training need. The three most common types of training are the following:
   a. Formal organized training with the company
   b. Educational institutional instruction
   c. Apprenticeship, or training on the job

3. The methods and procedures utilized in training. These vary widely, and considerable experience is available in printed form for consideration.

4. The organization required to conduct the requisite program. In report presentation, training organization should be discussed in this section only insofar as it deals with positions below the level generally dealt within detail in "Administrative Organization."

COMPENSATION
The investigator should determine whether the client compensation policy provides for the following:

1. Securing capable personnel. Generally, suitable employees can best be secured by offering a starting wage within the range representing the industry average for the position in question, rather than by emphasizing the value of the training and prestige attached to the particular job. In selecting experienced personnel, their experience is, obviously, a significant factor.

2. Providing incentives. In order to induce employees to put forth their best efforts, it is necessary to base their compensation on their achievement or contribution. Such an arrangement is also attractive from an expense control viewpoint because of the proportion of variable expense. The degree to which the compensation plan succeeds in measuring achievement will generally indicate its worth. Obviously, the more able workers prefer incentives because they provide rewards for superiority.

3. Promoting favorable employee relations. These can be achieved by:
    a. Observing minimum industry wage scales
    b. Paying increases over minimums for achievement
    c. Voluntary granting of increases
    d. Compensating at the time and in the form most convenient to the employee

4. Insuring proper cost ratios. A major department store problem, for example, is the development of a sales compensation plan which assures customer service (numbers of salespeople), adequate individual compensation, and a departmental sales cost ratio that is not excessive.

In considering client compensation policy, it is necessary to consider the policy relating to each type of personnel.

EMPLOYEE BENEFITS
Most satisfactory employee benefit activities generally relate to the following:

1. Improving employee working conditions
2. Aiding in maintaining employee physical well being through vacations, medical care, exercise facilities and the like
3. Assisting in providing social and recreational activities
4. Providing such financial benefits as sick benefits, pensions, group insurance and the like

It should be remembered that though sound employee benefit activities are worth while they cannot overcome or remove the effect of unsound compensation policy. A sound compensation policy is basic.

DISCHARGE
Properly employees should be discharged only under the following circumstances:

1. Change in client's policy or activity
2. Seasonal or cyclical fluctuation in operations

3. Inability or inefficiency of employee
4. Employee disability

The investigator should determine whether employees are discharged in such a manner that they will have a kindly and cordial feeling toward the client and will not damage the client's goodwill. To secure this result it is desirable to discharge employees in the following manner:

1. Tell employee of discharge and reasons for it in a frank and friendly manner.
2. Provide for employee finding new work, if possible. This can sometimes be done by temporary continuation of employment, discharge compensation, suggestions regarding possible employers and the like.

PUBLIC AND INDUSTRIAL RELATIONS
To a considerable degree public and industrial relations are one and the same because the client's relations with the public are through its employees. Consequently, the investigator should ascertain whether the client has sound policies relating to:

1. Employee organizations and unions
2. Handling employee grievances
3. Employee relations with the public

The client should have some provision for developing employee deportment when in contact with the public and employees should have a definite idea of the proper manner to present their employer to the public. This necessitates that client business objectives be sound and public-spirited and that the client have the confidence of its employees.

E. Financial policies

TOPICS TO BE CONSIDERED
The topics to be considered in a study of financial policies are:

1. Determination of financial requirements
2. Sources of capital
3. Control of capital
4. Protection of capital
5. Distribution of capital

The financial policies which should be adopted by any company are dependent upon its financial condition and requirements. The investigator, therefore, should not approach the financial policy study until after financial condition and requirements have been determined. This same statement is applicable, to a greater or lesser extent, to the study of all types of policies, because of the obvious limitations imposed by inadequate funds.

DETERMINATION OF FINANCIAL REQUIREMENTS
The investigator should appraise the client policy and methods utilized in coordination of the financial activities with all of the operating activities of the business. Consideration should be given to the policy and methods in determination of:

1. Basic requirements for fixed capital; that is, the capital required for investment in facilities of a permanent nature. In this connection, it is important to determine whether the facilities can best be obtained by making a fixed investment or by leasing and so on.

2. Basic working capital. Consideration should be given to the financial pattern of the business in this determination. Consideration should also be given to the effect of depression conditions upon the business, so as to properly emphasize the safety factor.

3. Extraordinary requirements, or additions to (1) and (2).

It is the opinion of our firm that the most effective means to determine the long and short term financial requirements is by means of a budgetary program. This point in the report, therefore, serves as an excellent place to sell a budget installation. The purpose of the long-term budget is to formalize the long-term planning of such items as expenditures for capital assets, readjustments in the capital structure, and the disposition of earnings. The purpose of the short-term budget is to establish a working financial program thoroughly coordinated with all of the operating plans of the company.

SOURCES OF CAPITAL
The sources from which capital may be obtained are the following:

1. *Earnings.* This has been the most conservative and least expensive means of obtaining funds in the case of relatively small companies. The cost of capital from this source has been increased by the tax on undistributed profits, and it is not possible to anticipate modifications in this legislation at the present time.

2. *Common stock.* The issuance of common stock will usually present the most conservative means of financing, although not necessarily the least expensive. Stockholders, obviously, are subject to the ups and downs of the business and must take "pot luck" with the enterprise.

3. *Preferred stock.* Preferred stock may be issued to present owners through "rights" (as may common stock also) or to the public. This stock may or may not have cumulative, participating or conversion privileges. The need for inclusion of one or more of these privileges is dependent upon the factors which are discussed subsequently.

4. *Fixed indebtedness.* In the case of companies which have large fixed capital requirements or where earnings remain at a sufficiently high rate to maintain interest and sinking fund requirements in times of depression, it is common practice to obtain capital through the issuance of long-term debt. Mortgage bonds can usually only be issued against real property, while debentures are often issued against other than real property and do not represent a mortgage on the property.

5. *Bank loans.* This source of capital is desirable when the indebtedness is of a seasonal or temporary nature.

6. *Other sources.* It is possible to secure capital requirements from other sources, such as finance companies, who make a practice of discounting long-term paper, commercial paper houses which discount comparatively short-term paper, and factors who purchase outstanding receivables and who assume responsibility for collections. These sources are available for financing receivables or in some cases for financing inventory.

In appraising the client policy regarding sources of capital the investigator should consider the following factors which to a great extent control the source:

1. *Financial pattern of the business.* This is the pattern revealed by a study of the comparative balance sheets and operating statements over a period of time, and comprises, specifically:
- **a.** Ratios of assets to liabilities, and assets and liabilities to net worth
- **b.** Ratios between assets, liabilities and net worth on the one side and sales volume, costs and net earnings on the other
- **c.** The changes in (a) and (b) during the courses of a fiscal year as well as during the longer period covering the ebb and flow of business depression and boom.

The investigator must be familiar with the types of financing prevalent in the industry studied and should obviously consider the size of the client company, as certain sources of capital are not open to small businesses.

2. *Use of capital.* In considering sources of capital it is important to consider the use to which capital is to be put. It is common practice, for example, to finance a large portion of fixed capital requirements by means of long-term obligations and to finance working capital requirements and a portion of fixed capital requirements through stock or other media. The existing financial structure of the company is a determining factor in this consideration.

3. *Cost of financing.* The investigator should determine the relative cost of the various media which can be used. It might be unwise, for example, to provide sufficient capital to meet season requirements through the issuance of high yield permanent financing when the temporary needs can be secured from other sources.

4. *Attendant risk.* The investigator should measure the risk involved in incurring obligations involving either fixed maturities or interest payments. In this connection it should be pointed out that many provisions written into indentures have been intended to protect the investor but have resulted in imposing obligations upon the company which actually impaired the security of the investor. It is desirable, therefore, to make the provisions of the indentures sufficiently flexible to permit their modification in times of stress. In the case of a sinking fund, for example, the obligation to retire bonds might be contingent upon the maintenance of a certain rate of earnings.

CONTROL OF USE OF CAPITAL

The investigator should ascertain whether the client has adapted sound policies governing the control of the use of capital. This requires a consideration of:

1. Whether capital is being used for the purposes intended
2. The trend in the ratio between fixed capital and working capital
3. The trend in the relationship of inventories, receivables and fixed assets to sales and profits

PROTECTION OF CAPITAL

The investigator should ascertain whether the client is making proper use of the following means of protecting capital:

1. *Insurance.* Insurable risks should be adequately covered either by insurance in outside companies or through the maintenance of adequate liquid reserves. The three major questions to be considered in this type of protection are:
- **a.** Should the risk be carried by the client or by an outside agency? Generally speaking, hazards that lend themselves to actuarial analysis are protected by insurance policies, while those which cannot be readily measured statistically are carried by the company.
- **b.** If the protection is to be purchased from an insurance company, what

phases should be covered by the policy?

    c. What insurance company should be selected to carry the risk? This involves consideration of such factors as cost, service and financial strength of the available insurance companies.

2. *Reserves.* Reserves should be established to provide adequately for the replacement of plant and equipment.

3. *Maintenance.* Adequate provision should be made for maintenance of plant and other facilities.

4. *Credit and collection policies.* Accounts receivable should be protected by sound credit and collection policies.

5. *Investments.* Excess funds should be conservatively invested.

DISTRIBUTION OF CAPITAL
The investigator should determine whether the client has adopted sound policies governing the distribution of capital in the form of dividends. This involves consideration of:

1. Present financial condition and financial requirements
2. Desirability of a stable dividend policy
3. Demands of investors
4. Legal requirements of federal and state statutes
5. General business outlook

IV. ADMINISTRATIVE ORGANIZATION

Topics to be considered
The study of a client's organization involves consideration of:

1. Present plan of organization
2. Classification of activities
3. Relationship between activities
4. Standards of organization

The typical report presentation of this subject is outlined at the end of this section.

Present plan of organization
The investigator should determine the plan of the client's present administrative organization by:

1. Observation
2. Inquiry

These findings should be set forth in chart form and this chart should be checked with the chief executive. Once the chart on present organization has been approved by the client chief executives it becomes the basis for the balance of the organization study.

These factors should be considered in studying administrative organization:

1. What activities must be undertaken to achieve the objectives outlined by client's policies?

2. How should these activities be grouped and classified for purposes of administration?

3. What relationship should exist between these various groups and classifications?

4. How can these groups of activities best be coordinated?

5. How can these groups of activities best be administered?

Classification of activities

To determine the activities to be provided for in the plan of administrative organization, it is necessary to review client policies, inasmuch as organization is the plan by means of which activities necessary for execution of policies are administered.

Once requisite client activities have been determined, they should be classified in a manner that will permit effective management. Most significant classifications are those by:

1. Products
2. Processes
3. Territories
4. Types of customers
5. Functions

Relationship between activities

Groups and classes of activities should be related on the basis of the following:

1. Line authority, which is the common relationship between the employee and his superior. The executive with line authority has complete responsibility for the direction, supervision and control of his subordinates except in cases of special reservation. Similarly the subordinate is responsible to his superior for all matters except those specifically reserved.

2. Functional authority, which is the authority exercised by the executive who prescribes *how* certain activities should be performed. For example, the controller may be responsible for prescribing *how* the branch house clerk should prepare certain reports for the home office, hence he has functional authority over the clerk in this regard. On the other hand, the branch house manager is responsible for having the reports prepared and therefore has line authority over the clerk.

3. Staff relationship, which is that relationship between an executive and a subordinate who is responsible for research and study of certain problems confronting the executive. Staff relationship does not provide authority and consequently staff men are without authority unless it is expressly provided. An industrial engineer, for example, customarily acts in staff capacity.

4. Coordinating Committees, which provide a relationship necessary between executives of common standing who are responsible for definitely interrelated activities. Budgets, operating programs, financing and the like generally provide a need for a relationship of this sort between the heads of departments involved. Coordinating committees should be formally organized and recognized and should have definite responsibilities. Authority is generally best delegated to individual members of these committees rather than to the committee as a whole, for practical reasons.

Organization standards

Once activities have been determined and classified on the bases above, a tentative plan of organization should be blocked out and checked against the following standards:

1. Has adequate provision been made for all activities?
2. Have activities been grouped and classified logically?
3. Has definite responsibility for each group of activities been assigned?
4. Has sufficient responsibility been assigned to subordinates?
5. Are responsibility and authority coextensive?
6. Has proper provision been made for the effective control of individuals with authority and responsibility?
7. Have the subordinates reporting to any one executive been limited to a reasonable number?

8. Are subordinates responsible to only one executive on the basis of "line authority?"

9. Does the plan clearly distinguish between line and functional authority?

10. Have adequate means for coordinating various groups of activites been provided?

Once the proposed plan of organization has been tested against these standards it should be presented to the client for comment and approval. Obviously the entire organization study should be undertaken in close relationship with the client for these reasons:

1. So that the investigator is familiar with the client's present organization

2. So that the client will accept the proposed plan as an improvement

3. So that the client's executives will begin to think in terms of the organization plan

Method of presentation

In preparing an organization report either separately or as a section of a general survey, the following method of presentation is most suitable:

1. Indicate the objective of a plan of administrative organization

2. Outline the client's present plan of organization in both chart and narrative form

3. Point out the limitations of (2) on the basis of (1)

4. Outline the proposed plan of organization in both chart and narrative form

5. Point out the advantages of (4) over (2)

6. Define the responsibilities of the executive to fill each position provided for by the organization plan. Even though detailed responsibility definitions may not be required in a general survey report, it is generally advisable to present a definition of the general responsibilities of executives who are to fill positions not called for in *the old organization* plan of the client.

Detailed discussions of "organization" are contained in the Training Manual. In report presentation, caution should be exercised to avoid duplication of the discussion of Organization as provided for under "Policies" and in this section.

V. EXECUTIVE PERSONNEL

Objective

The objective of this study is to appraise client personnel of executive calibre. It is important to note this restriction on the type of personnel considered in this study as over against Personnel Policies where we were concerned with personnel in the broad sense including labor and the like.

No phase of a general survey (or other engagement which includes this topic) is of greater importance to the client, to the individual client executive, and to the reputation of our Firm than that dealing with the appraisal of executive personnel. While it is relatively easy to reduce to writing a method of appraisal, it is extremely difficult, especially during the generally limited course of a professional engagement, to appraise individuals with certainty. The investigators, therefore, should exercise extreme caution in arriving at conclusions. It is unpardonable to recommend the dismissal of an executive when any element of doubt exists as to the soundness of the move. No appraisal of any sort should be submitted, furthermore, until at least three investigators of partner or senior rank are in *complete* agreement, an agreement reached as the result of independent appraisals.

Sound appraisal of personnel is dependent upon:

1. Proper standards for judging personnel

2. Proper methods for applying these standards

We discuss the manner of report presentation at the end of this section.

Standards of appraisal

In appraising executive personnel the investigator should ascertain whether the individual has:

1. A successful experience record
2. An analytical mind
3. A logical mind
4. An open mind, yet not lacking in decisiveness
5. Knowledge of the field
6. Ability to work both harmoniously and effectively with associates
7. Ability to direct and supervise subordinates
8. Ability to progress

Standards (2) to (8), inclusive, in all likelihood combine to a greater or lesser extent, where (1) is favorable. The investigator should stress standard (1), however, because of the extreme difficulty of measuring the individual in terms of the other standards. The others are important, however, especially as the level of executive authority increases.

Application methods

The above standards can be applied in appraising executives by the following methods:

1. Studying the results achieved by the executive
2. Observing the executive at work, especially in his dealings with subordinates and as a member of conferences
3. Interviewing the executive
4. Determining the attitude of associates and subordinates toward the executive

Report presentation

Each appraisal should be presented fairly, courageously and frankly. Each executive should be appraised individually in the report in light of the above standards.

Appraisals should be limited to important executives and should be as brief as possible. This is important because lengthy appraisals, even though generally favorable, may include minor points that will annoy the executive in question, with resulting unnecessary ill-will toward the Firm.

Wherever dismissal or change of position is indicated as a result of the appraisal, the investigator must make definite recommendations in that regard and either suggest candidates for the vacated position, if that is possible, or offer to assist in procuring needed executive personnel.

Of equal importance to the presentation of appraisals when dismissal is necessary is the presentation of recommendations as to the timing of dismissals. Obviously chaos might result if the client dismissed two or three major executives the day following receipt of the report, and before suitably trained substitutes were available.

In many cases it is wise to present this section of the report as a supplement in view of the confidential nature of the material.

VI. FACILITIES

Topics to be considered

In order to appraise client facilities from an operating point of view it is necessary to give consideration to:

1. Location
2. Design and capacity
3. Layout

Location

The soundness of the location of facilities should be appraised in terms of:

1. Location with respect to the market. It is necessary to determine the extent to which the market must be adjacent to a business of the type being studied. For example, a department store must be located in a shopping center while certain manufacturers may well be far removed from their markets. Generally, the geographical distribution of the market should be studied with reference to:

    a. The effect of transportation costs on client competitive position
    b. Competitive distribution cost position
    c. Competitive distribution service position

Consider the use of branch warehouses in overcoming disadvantages indicated by this study.

2. Sources of raw materials, in particular regarding:

    a. Availability
    b. Assembly costs of raw materials
    c. Soundness of location of converting, fabricating and finishing plants with respect to their raw material. Sources from the cost, administration and storage requirements viewpoints.

3. Labor supply, regarding:

    a. Availability of necessary labor, skilled and common
    b. Comparative wage rates
    c. Union situation
    d. Provision for off-season employment in other local industries

4. Transportation and communication as it relates to:

    a. Inbound freight, either rail, truck or water
    b. Outbound freight, either rail, truck or water
    c. Telephone and telegraph
    d. Mail service, including air mail
    e. Passenger service

5. Local legislation and political attitude as it relates to:

    a. Taxation
    b. Labor
    c. Conservation of natural resources
    d. "Foreign" corporations
    e. Industrial nuisances

6. Climatic and physical conditions relating to:

    a. Effect of climate on material, processes, facilities and personnel
    b. Disposal of wastes
    c. Land used

7. Power

8. Prestige value (customer acceptance)

9. Special inducements

In recommending changes in location of facilities, consider:

1. Estimated costs of making changes
2. Effect of changes on long-term production schedule
3. The time required to make the changes
4. Effect of necessary expenditures on client financial condition and program

Design and capacity

It is necessary for the investigator to determine the adequacy of the design and capacity of:

1. *Buildings.* Client buildings should be appraised regarding:
   a. Relative advantages of the type of construction
   b. The effect on operations of such characteristics as head room, column spacing, heating, ventilating, air conditioning, floor surface, lighting, and interbuilding transportation
   c. The appearance as affected by maintenance, painting, and housekeeping
   d. The costs of heat, light, and power as related to the nature of the building
   e. Cost of maintenance as related to the building and the client maintenance program
   f. Cost of insurance as affected by the type of construction nature of the building and the maintenance program
   e. Suitability for expansion

2. *Production machinery and equipment.* Production machinery and equipment should be studied with reference to:
   a. Suitability in terms of type, capacity, and economy; on the basis of the normal requirements; seasonal and peak load requirements; and provision for reasonable growth
   b. The effect of age and obsolescence on performance and capacity
   c. Costs of power, compressed air, process steam, and the like as affected by operating conditions
   d. Costs of maintenance as affected by present conditions and maintenance practices

3. *Material handling and storage equipment* which should be appraised on the same basis as production machinery and equipment

4. *Boiler, power and other service equipment* which should be appraised on the same basis as production machinery and equipment
   Recommendations with regard to changes in the design and capacity of facilities should be based on the same considerations as suggested under "Location."

Layout

To determine the adequacy of the layout of client facilities, it is necessary to consider:

1. Plant site and the arrangement of buildings, as they provide for:
   a. Natural flow of production
   b. Orderly receipt and dispatch of materials and products
   c. Controlled access to the premises
   d. Economic use of available ground area
   e. Provision for possible growth

2. Arrangement of departments which should be studied with reference to:
   a. The basis on which operations are separated into departments. Common bases are: Functional use of equipment; straight line flow of production; utilization of common supervision and facilities; and physical limitations of the buildings
   b. The soundness of present departmental arrangement from point of view of: General plant supervision; material handling; natural flow of production; and economic distribution of power and other utilities

3. Arrangement of machinery and equipment within departments on the basis of:
   a. Floor area required
   b. Adequacy of provision for: Natural unimpeded flow of production with minimum handling; economical and convenient storage of raw materials; economic and convenient storage of work-in-process; and supervision of inspection
   c. Economical utilization of the area provided

4. Arrangement and location of service departments which should be studied with reference to:

a. Economical and convenient delivery of the service to point of use
b. Floor area required
c. Economic utilization of the area provided

Recommendations with regard to change in layout of facilities should be based on the considerations suggested under "Location."

A more detailed outline of a facilities study is included in the Training Manual. In report presentation, utilize the headings in this section of the outline insofar as possible.

VII.   CONTROLS AND PROCEDURES

Introductory comment

Provision has been made under "Policies" for the discussion of certain controls and procedures which relate to:

1. Sales (not sales order procedure)
2. Production
3. Purchasing
4. Personnel

Discussion of these controls and procedures should be at those points, however, only when the treatment is general. Detailed discussion of these controls and procedures belongs in this section. In survey report presentation, a serious production control problem should be indicated under "Policies," and reference should be made to the detailed discussion in this section.

Scope

A study of controls and procedures should be a critical analysis of each control and procedure to determine whether or not the procedure is necessary and whether it produces the desired results at a cost which is commensurate with the value received from these results. A logical phase of the study, obviously, is to determine whether some provision has been made for all essential controls and procedures.

The controls and procedures generally studied relate to:

1. Order handling, particularly regarding:
   a. Sales statistics
   b. Sales order
   c. Credit and collections
   d. Production planning and scheduling

2. Material procurement, particularly regarding:
   a. Purchasing
   b. Receiving
   c. Stores control
   d. Accounts payable

3. Labor, particularly regarding:
   a. Timekeeping
   b. Payroll
   c. Personnel

4. Delivery of goods, particularly regarding:
   a. Shipping
   b. Freight and traffic
   c. Billing
   d. Accounts receivable

5. Accounting, particularly regarding:
    a. Cost accounting
    b. General accounting, including budgets
    c. Treasurer and cashier

6. Miscellaneous, including:
    a. Statistical (tabulating)
    b. Office services
    c. Other

In analyzing the control and procedure problem, it is essential that consideration be given to:

1. Client policies
2. Client organization
3. Clerical personnel
4. Office facilities
5. Clerical methods

Changes recommended elsewhere in the report regarding the first four factors should obviously be considered in making control and procedure recommendations. Suggestions as to improvements in clerical methods to increase efficiency or reduce cost should be presented in this section.

An outline of the Firm approach to procedure studies is contained in the Training Manual.

Report presentation

Recommended controls and procedures should be presented in report form in the following sequence:

1. Statement of objectives
2. Analysis of present practice (the amount of detail increasing in proportion to the distance from the routine of the report recipient)
3. Analysis of limitations of present practice
4. Recommended practice (in detail, by steps)
5. Statement of anticipated benefits (including savings)
6. Program for realizing anticipated benefits

In general survey reports where the necessity arises for a long section dealing with controls and procedures, this section of the report should be submitted in the form of a supplement. The problems, recommendations and expected benefits, however, should be summarized in the Letter of Transmittal included in the major volume.

VIII.   FINANCIAL CONDITION

Topics to be considered

In the general survey study of client financial conditions it is necessary to consider:

1. Present financial condition as reflected by the balance sheet
2. Operating results as reflected by the profit and loss statement

Financial condition

In appraising client present financial condition it is necessary that the investigator:

1. Present a balance sheet as of the latest date possible which analyzes assets and

liabilities sufficiently to bring to the attention of the reader all significant items. For example, if the officers of the corporation owe it money, the amount of their obligations should be shown as a separate item. If the inventory is composed of some obsolete materials, this should be set up as a separate item on the balance sheet. The investigator should have as his objective, the presentation of a balance sheet which will bring to the attention of the reader of the report all items to which you think he should direct his attention.

2. Show the trend in financial condition by presenting comparative balance sheets for a period of three or more years. Arrange these in form so the reader can quickly see the significant trends.

3. Present an analysis of the balance sheet by discussing each asset and liability item, calling attention to any facts which you think should be significant to the reader. Give particular attention to the following items:
- **a.** Receivables
- **b.** Inventories
- **c.** Current liabilities or fixed liabilities which mature in the near future
- **d.** Contingent liabilities

4. If the analysis made in (3) indicates that adjustments should be made on the balance sheet presented in (1), present an adjusted balance sheet and show a comparison between this and the original balance sheet. Call attention to any significant changes which are shown by this comparison.

5. Present a comparison of working capital for a period of three or more years and explain any significant changes.

6. Present a statement of Application of Funds for as long a period as it seems feasible and desirable, and show the relationship between this statement and changes in working capital as shown in (5).

7. Present a summary of your conclusion with reference to the present financial condition of the firm.

Operating results

In appraising client operating results it is necessary that the investigator:

1. Present a statement of Income and Expense for the last year or for the period since the end of the last fiscal year, if this is sufficiently long to be of value.

2. Present comparative statements of Income and Expense for the past three or more years.

3. Analyze the major items of income and expense and discuss the trends which seem to be significant. Present, if possible, the reasons for favorable or unfavorable trends shown by these comparative statements.

4. Present, if it seems desirable, analyses of income and expense items by means of supplementary statements. For example, it may be desirable to present a detailed analysis of sales in order to show the reasons for important trends in sales volume. It may also be necessary to present analysis of manufacturing costs in order to show the reasons for trends in these costs.

5. Present a summary of your conclusions with reference to the operating results of the firm. In making this summary present in logical order the facts which you think the recipient of a report would consider most important.

It is important that all comments on financial condition be set forth in a readable form so as to assure maximum reader understanding and interest. It should be remembered that many report recipients are not financial analysts and consequently our comments should be non-technical. This section of the report is not intended to be an audit.

IX. FINANCIAL REQUIREMENTS

Section scope

In the case of financing studies and those general surveys where the client is confronted with strained finances, an analysis of financial requirements is very important and deserves detailed consideration. A suitable analysis requires that the investigator:

1. Prepare a forecast of future operations by means of budgets which will provide the following:
   a. Estimated income and expense by months for one year
   b. Estimates of cash receipts and disbursements by months for one year
   c. Estimated balance sheet for six months and twelve months in the future

In preparing these budgets give careful consideration to the following:
   a. Sales possibilities in terms of the conclusions arrived at in the preceding sections of this report, with reference to the outlook for the company, sales policy, and sales organization
   b. Expense reductions. The investigator should carefully analyze all expenses in terms of the proposed sales program and seek to secure as substantial reductions as possible.
   c. The relation of volume to unit costs and, consequently, to sales prices

2. Present a comparison between the estimates of income and expense and the income and expense of past periods by giving comparative income and expense statements for three or more years. Discuss the important trends indicated by these comparative statements.

3. The information secured by these budgets should be summarized to show the following:
   a. Whether the firm can be placed on a profitable basis
   b. If it cannot be placed on a profitable basis immediately, whether it can be placed on a basis where it can operate without additional cash
   c. If additional cash is required, the probable amount necessary, and whether it is believed future operations will justify the expenditure of these funds
   d. Whether future operations of the company will increase or decrease the assets of the firm
   e. If these operations will decrease the assets, determine whether there are compensating advantages in continuing the operations of the firm which will offset the disadvantage of this decrease

This section of the report serves as a logical point to stress the importance of budgets. Development and installation of a system of budgetary control is one of the most logical follow-up engagements to sell during a general survey study.

A careful reading of the General Survey Outline reveals why McKinsey was reluctant to write it: it is essentially a checklist of the areas the consultant should explore and the information the consultant should seek. Only in the discussion of organization standards does it contain a normative model against which the data can be compared. The outline suggests what information the consultant needs in order to make judgments; it does not guide those judgments and thus there is the possibility of the outline being used in a rote manner.

McKinsey recognized this danger and tried to guard against it by providing intensive experiences for his junior consultants. Moreover, he saw precept and example as the means of training younger men. Neukom observed:

Mac, being a pedagogue, was very much concerned with training in his firm from the very beginning. One of the things he gave to the profession is his concern for training and some actual effort in that direction. There were regular training meetings, and there was on-the-job training. There was an effort on the part of the senior members of the firm to give the junior members an opportunity by exposing them to the situations, as they came along, in the various companies we were dealing with at the time.[5]

Neukom went on to reflect about his own training under McKinsey, and how young men were thrown into action at an early date.

Well, I remember my first piece of work. Actually, I went on the payroll September 10, 1934. The night before, at 11:45, I got on the Motor City Special on the Michigan Central Railroad to go to Detroit on my initial assignment in Detroit. I was meeting Bill Newman and Marvin Bower who were already on the job. . . . I was added to that study team. We had been retained by Borden's to come up with a new and imaginative approach to delivery of their dairy products residentially and this we did. We developed a creative approach to it by getting a good feel for what was going on. We rode the route wagons for some weeks. We spent some time learning the economics of the business and then came up with what we thought were interesting and dramatic approaches to residential delivery.

We designed equipment, a new type of truck, for this purpose. We worked around the general concept that the trouble with the present delivery system was that the driver was expected to do too many things. He delivered the merchandise, drove the truck, acted as credit manager, collected the accounts, and he was supposed to get new business. After the day's run was over he was supposed to dress up, put on a white shirt and go out and call on two ladies who were not taking milk, to see if he couldn't get them on his route.

This was a real decathlon requirement. So we decided to split the thing up and have some people concentrate on sales and credit and we designed a special delivery truck that took a three-man crew. One on the driver's seat and two working on runways on each side of the truck; reloading their carriers while the truck was moving and then jumping off and making three or four houses on this side and three or four houses on that side. The driver also loaded carriers when he had time. Of course all of that was in the days when home delivery was dense, and before women began buying their milk and cream from supermarkets.

Mac used to do a very good job of throwing junior fellows into these situations. I remember one of our other important client situations was Marshall Field's, where he later became chairman of the board. One of our early studies was the Davis store and after we'd spent some months taking a look at the store, we had a team meeting in the conference room in the office and Mac turned to the team and said, "I wish you'd tell me what you'd do with this store if you owned it." Well this gave us the full question to answer. I mean that's what we had been studying all this time. This wasn't a partial assignment, this was the whole thing. What would you do with the store? I said I'd sell it to Goldblatts. His eyes sparkled and he said "that's an idea" and within a year he did. As far as I know Goldblatts still have what was the Davis store on State Street.

That sort of thing happened every now and then. He'd throw the whole thing at you and let you chew on it – not often in front of clients; more often in front of just the study team. But he erred on the side of maximum exposure for the junior fellows rather than minimum exposure.

For if he was going to an important client meeting, he'd bring along as many of the study teams as he could without cluttering up the room, having the client say, "Boy, this is pretty expensive stuff, with all these guys with taxi meters running all the time."[6]

The General Survey Outline has two weaknesses. The first relates to the lack of normative standards, which means the consultant has to determine them. If he happens to have an excellent mind and the power of synthesis, this is not a problem, but if he does not, the outline cannot compensate for his deficiencies. The outline, then, does not teach anything more than an orderly procedure.

In fact, the outline is essentially a guide to diagnosis. The competent consultant can use it to design a normative model of the company he is studying. The process of developing the data called for helps him see the whole picture and establish that model, as well as measure the distance between the model and what he observes for each aspect of the business.

A second weakness of the outline as originally conceived was its complexity and length. Neukom considers that "total devotion to the General Survey Outline can result in somewhat unbalanced reports because some areas are covered in great detail and others only broadly. ... In part, this problem was resolved in many client reports by first having a summary chapter that covered in limited detail the matters that were of interest to most readers."[7] The basic soundness of the outline, however, has been proven again and again. Perhaps the fact that it is still the basic structure of the seventh edition of Newman's book is proof enough of its value.

The Marshall Field Case

Another interesting way to gain insight into McKinsey's consulting style is to review his assignment for Marshall Field and Company. McKinsey was called in to consult for Marshall Field in 1935. At that time it was the largest department store in the Midwest, with eighty-four years of accumulated tradition. *Fortune* magazine claimed, "You ask any good citizen what are the seven wonders of Chicago, and the first three that come to mind are likely be the stockyards, Michigan Boulevard and Marshall Field's."[8]

In the thirties, Marshall Field's was so famous that it would not condescend to have its name over the door. *Fortune* described its main store as follows:

There was a time, not many years ago [in the 1920s] when Field's had the biggest volume of any department store in the world. . . . It was then —and is now [in 1936] a great, square, gray-granite block of a building, with four tall monoliths guarding its main entrance on State Street, with arches, guilded gateways, fountains, and panelled walls inside, an ornate glass dome designed by Louis Tiffany over one of its two vast, galleried light wells. Its sixty-seven show windows are stately and dull. Marshall Field's displays few prices. It caters frankly to that prosperous stratum of respectable society which has lost its solidarity since the war [World War I], and it sells the best goods that can be sold.[9]

Marshall Field's State Street store was and still is upper class — a symbol of style, quality, and sophisticated merchandising. During the thirties, despite the Depression, it took high mark-ups and maintained its image. But the Marshall Field empire was more than the main department store. It included two other retail stores, twenty-four textile mills in the South, the Chicago Merchandise Mart, the largest dry goods businesses in the United States, and a department store on State Street in Chicago known as the Davis Store.

By tradition, Marshall Field was a wholesaler. The founder, Marshall Field, was a wholesale merchant who instilled in his executives a wholesaler's tradition. The company had both wholesale and retail business, however, and the relative importance of the retail segment was obscured. Beginning around 1900, the wholesale business began to decline. By 1927, it was losing money, but the losses were more than offset by the profits from retailing. By 1931, earnings from the retail store could no longer cover the losses from the wholesale business, and the company lost $5,000,000. The following year, it lost $8,000,000. In 1934, the retail store made a profit of $2,450,000 but the company as a whole lost $166,000.

The Field directors met in January 1935 to consider this situation. Dominated by the company's traditions, they recognized that they needed outside help to deal with their problem. They called McKinsey in as consultant. By 1935, McKinsey's reputation was well established. His company had already worked for the Chicago Corporation, an investment firm in which Marshall Field III was interested, and Field had been favorably impressed. Hence, when the board of directors of Marshall Field decided to retain a management consultant, they immediately called McKinsey.

McKinsey agreed to study the business and see if he could find what was wrong. He came in with a staff of twelve and began interviewing. Within four months McKinsey gave the Field directors an oral report in which he advised them to get rid of the wholesale division. This recommendation was particularly drastic since the wholesale division had been the traditional core of Marshall Field's. In addition, it was a large part of the company: it accounted for around a third of the company's annual sales, and it employed approximately a thousand persons. In his subsequent reports, McKinsey also recommended concentrating on the retail business and selling off the Fieldcrest Mills and the Merchandise Mart.

On April 27, 1935, McKinsey submitted a brief written report to H. P. Shedd, vice-president of Marshall Field. The style of the report was typical of McKinsey. First, he wasted no words and kept to the facts. Second, he organized his thinking in outline form. Third, he cited his research to give authority to the report. Finally, he stated his conclusions in a tentative way, using formulations such as "we find" and "we desire the benefit of your thinking."

The board of directors of Marshall Field accepted McKinsey's recommendations. Once they did so, they had to find someone who would implement them. They decided to go to an outsider for the first time in the company's history to ensure freedom from the Field tradition. Thus they offered McKinsey the position of chairman of the board of directors.

Notes

1. Newman, *Business Policies.*
2. Interview, April 11, 1973.
3. Interview, July 1, 1976.
4. Neukom, *McKinsey Memoirs,* p. 12.

5. Interview, October 3, 1975.

6. Ibid.

7. Ibid.

8. "Marshall Field," *Fortune* 14, no. 4 (October 1936): 79.

9. Ibid.

Chapter V

Precepts and Caveats for Managers

The preceding chapters provide a general understanding of McKinsey the man, McKinsey the management theorist, and McKinsey the consultant. They paint McKinsey as a pragmatic, objective, and systematic thinker. His contributions to management centered on budgetary control, accounting, managerial accounting, and an approach to business policy that emphasized integrating management functions and seeing the organization in a holistic framework. In both his writing and his consulting, he insisted on the importance of obtaining facts, ordering them, and remaining objective and systematic in using them to pursue management goals. Above all, McKinsey's work was dominated by a rational approach—logic, facts, and the proper flow of information should solve any problem.

Probably the best way to summarize McKinsey's ideas is to present them as precepts and caveats for management. Although, he never presented them in this manner and it may be presumptuous to do so here, a careful reading of his writings does enable one to deduce a set of guidelines for managing.

The twelve guidelines that follow represent more than a summary of what has been discussed, for they also involve applying some of McKinsey's general ideas. Moreover, they include concepts that do not fit readily into the preceding text. These guidelines start with the broader concepts and gradually narrow to specific topics. Throughout, a top management point of view is taken. The objective is to present a series of guidelines for top managers which are derived from McKinsey's writings.

1. Remember that the chief executive's job is as much external as internal. This means that the executive must constantly monitor the economic, political, and social environment for changes and events that will affect his firm. Consequently, he must develop a mental set that will enable him to relate a wide variety of data to his firm and its future.

2. Differentiate between policy formation and administration. Generally, broad and general policies such as the kind of business, the size of the business, major capital expenditures, and the appointment of top-level personnel should be decided by the board of directors, based on the recommendations of the president or chief executive. Administration of these policies is a function of the chief executive officer. In other words, "the President of the Company, when he acts as the chief executive officer, has little time to give to constructive thinking and such thinking is necessary for the formulation of effective policies."[1]

3. Encourage the board of directors to audit the activities of the firm. This allows the board "to judge the efficiency of the executives whose selection it has approved." It also tends to ensure that long-run policy decisions are compatible with the existing organization. To facilitate this audit procedure, "the Board should receive at regular intervals budgets showing the program of the company as a whole. At the end of each accounting period it should receive statements showing a comparison between the budget for each period and the actual results." Furthermore, to ensure a better understanding of the firm "it is desirable that the members of the Board who are not executives [of the company] should also become acquainted with all of the important activities of the company by personal observation." This not only improves the functioning of the board of directors, it also "produces a desirable psychological effect on the members of the organization."[2]

4. Recognize that the chief executives in charge of specialized units will tend to develop a point of view limited to their areas, whether they be sales, production, or personnel. Under such circumstances conflict is inherent, and the president must maintain an integrated point of view and coordinate the adverse activities of the business.

5. Establish committees to facilitate coordination of the various departments. "For example, there may be a sales committee, composed of the sales manager, production

manager, the personnel manager, the controller and the treasurer. ... In the same way a committee may be established to pass upon each of the major divisions of the business."[3]

6. Have clear and concise major policies. Such policies are "plans of action based upon certain assumed conditions."[4] This means that not only must policies be formulated carefully, but they must also be communicated to the organization.

7. Remember that the world is dynamic and changing. This means that policies must be adjusted frequently to fit the changing situation. This in turn requires the president to keep up with the facts. He should maintain a research outlook so that he will know what is happening and be able to adjust, adapt, and otherwise change policies to meet changing conditions.[5]

8. Delegate responsibility and authority but centralize control. Formal authority and responsibility should be delegated as far down the organization as possible. "Most men work best when they feel they are working as individuals, so the successful executive must strive to give the specialists he supervises such freedom that their initiative will not be restricted unduly, but at the same time, the executive must exercise such control as to provide sufficient coordination to prevent wasted effort and ill effects from conflicting activities of these specialists: the greater degree to which the controls he uses are intangible and flexible the more effective his supervision will be."[6]

9. Take charge of "fixing responsibility on the members of the organization for executing the policies of the business," and "checking up on the organization to see that these responsibilities are properly executed." Furthermore, "it is desirable that the chief executive present to all members of the organization a clear picture of what the organization is. The most effective method of doing this is by means of organization charts and manuals."[7]

10. Recognize the limitations and weaknesses of the organization chart:

"It is merely an administrative device which enables an executive to see the men who are responsible for performing the activities of the company.

There is no one kind of organization chart that is right ... there is no ideal form of organization. Every business has to work out its own organization in terms of its particular problems and personnel. ... It is also important that we remember that an organization chart must be changing continuously because the organization will be changing continuously."[8]

11. Remember that one of the useful devices for communicating policies, delegating responsibilities, and maintaining control is a well-designed and well-administered budgeting system. This means that the chief executive must have a budget committee to aid in the coordination required for the budget, must educate his organization as to policies and budgets, and must have a prompt flow of accurate data to facilitate evaluation and control.

12. Adopt the viewpoint that the main control is self-control. If individuals are to be responsible, they need to want to accomplish their delegated tasks. For they determine with how much enthusiasm and effort they will contribute to the specialized activities which constitute the organization. Hence, it is important to motivate individuals. McKinsey saw this as part of leadership, and to achieve it he advised the manager to (1) develop empathy by determining what the individual wants and not trying to change him, (2) stimulate thinking and educate, but not seek credit for what he has done, and (3) remember "the elementary principle of pedagogy — the student must teach himself rather than being taught by the instructor."[9]

Using these precepts as a guide, it follows that the chief executive should have lower levels of management participate in the administration of policies. For example, in establishing budgets, those who will be responsible for specific aspects of performance should be consulted when standards are being determined.[10] McKinsey advised the manager to assume that most individuals want to better themselves: if there is an explicit, tangible reward system, one tends to get greater efficiency. McKinsey also encouraged "training which will develop the thinking of the employee so that he may have a proper appreciation of the significance of the incentives offered to him."[11] In other words, create in the employee a desire for the rewards offered by the firm.

The above are some general guides derived from the writings of James Oscar McKinsey. In a sense, they contribute to a handbook mentality on how to manage. This is not what we intend, for McKinsey worshipped sound thinking. He saw each firm as unique, and continually reiterated that there are few general solutions. Most important, McKinsey believed that ultimately it is wisdom and good judgment that make a manager successful.

Notes

1. McKinsey, *Budgeting Technique.*

2. James O. McKinsey, *Functions of Boards of Directors, Board Committees and Officers,* General Management Series, no. 82 (New York: American Management Association, 1929), p. 70.

3. Ibid., p. 13.

4. McKinsey, *Adjusting Policies,* p. 3.

5. James O. McKinsey, *Organization Problems under Present Conditions,* General Management Series, no. 127 (New York: American Management Association, 1936), p. 10.

6. Ibid.

7. McKinsey, *Functions of Boards of Directors,* p. 11.

8. McKinsey, *Sixteen Trends,* p. 23

9. McKinsey, *Budgeting Technique,* p. 71.

10. Ibid., p. 72.

11. McKinsey, *Organization Problems,* p. 14.

Appendix A

The Principal Writings of James O. McKinsey

Accounting Lectures. Cincinnati: South-Western Publishing Co., 1920.

Accounting Principles. Cincinnati: South-Western Publishing Co., 1929. Revised in 1931, then in 1935 with Howard Noble, who revised it again in 1939, and then in 1944 for the U.S. Armed Forces Institute.

Adjusting Policies to Meet Changing Conditions. General Management Series, no. 116. New York: American Management Association, 1932.

"Boards of Directors, Board Committees, and Officers," In *Handbook of Business Administration,* edited by W. J. Donald. New York: McGraw-Hill, 1931.

Bookkeeping and Accounting. Vol. 1. Cincinnati: South-Western Publishing Co., 1920. McKinsey revised the book in 1926 and 1931, and Edwin Piper revised it in 1938, 1939, and 1950. Vol.2 — Series B, 1921; revised 2nd ed., 1926; 3rd ed., 1932.

Budgetary Control. New York: Ronald Press, 1922.

"Budgetary Control." In *Management's Handbook,* edited by L. P. Alford. New York: Ronald Press, 1924. Written with James Palmer.

Budgetary Control for Business. Boston: Bureau of Commercial and Industrial Affairs, Boston Chamber of Commerce, 1920.

Budgeting Technique. Annual Convention Series, no. 51. New York: American Management Association, 1926.

Business Administration. Cincinnati: South-Western Publishing Co., 1924.

Cases and Problems No. 3, Organization and Methods of the Walworth Manufacturing Company. Chicago: University of Chicago Press, 1922.

Controlling the Finances of a Business. New York: Ronald Press, 1923. Written with Stuart P. Meech.

Coordination of Sales, Production and Finance. AMA Sales Executive Series, no. 9. New York: American Management Association, 1924.

"Effect of Mergers on Marketing Production and Administrative Problems." *Management Review* 18 (February 1929): 39−46.

Federal Income and Excess Profits Tax Laws. Cincinnati: South-Western Publishing Co., 1920.

"The Finance Committee." In *Handbook of Business Administration,* edited by W. J. Donald, New York: McGraw-Hill, 1931.

Financial Management: An Outline of Its Principles and Problems. 2 vols. Chicago: American Technical Society, 1922. Revised in 1935 with Willard J. Graham.

Formulation of a Financial Budget. Pamphlet no. 10. Boston: Committee on Business and Finance, Bureau of Commercial and Industrial Affairs, Boston Chamber of Commece, 1921.

Functions of Boards of Directors, Board Committees and Officers. General Management Series, no. 82. New York: American Management Association, 1929.

"Interpretation of the 1918 Revenue Law." A series of lectures delivered before the Chicago chapter of the American Institute of Banking. n.d.

Managerial Accounting. Vol. 1. Chicago: University of Chicago Press, 1924. The second volume was never published.

Organization Problems under Present Conditions. General Management Series, no. 127. New York: American Management Association, 1936.

Principles of Accounting. Chicago: University of Chicago Press, 1920. Written with A. C. Hodges.

Reorganizing Executive and Financial Management Functions. Financial Executive Series, no. 5. New York: American Management Association, 1925.

Sixteen Trends in Management Organization. Annual Convention Series, no. 33. New York: American Management Association, 1926.

Social Responsibility of Private Enterprise. General Management Series, no. 130. New York: American Management Association, 1937.

Successful Departmental Budgeting. Annual Convention Series, no. 65. New York: American Management Association, 1928. Written with W. S. Clithero.

"Teacher's Manual for Accounting Principles." Cincinnati: South-Western Publishing Co., 1931.

Appendix B

McKinsey's Illustration of a Manual of Budgeting Procedures

To show concretely the possible contents of a manual on budgetary procedure, there is given below the manual of a manufacturing company. The company has sales of about $6,000,000 a year. Part of the product of the company is sold direct to the customer, while the remainder is sold to merchants. Branches are used to market part of the goods.

The president, who is also treasurer, does not reside in the city where the company is located but maintains an active interest in its affairs. The assistant treasurer is general manager; the other principal executives are the sales manager and works manager. The assistant to the general manager serves as office manager and head of the accounting and statistical departments. The company's accounting period is four weeks and its budget period is three accounting periods.

I. Organization for Budgetary Control

1. The President

The President of the Company is to have direct control of all matters pertaining to the budgetary program. All officers to whom authority is delegated in this manual are acting as his agents and are responsible to him for the proper performance of the duties delegated to them. In all cases of disagreement between departments with reference to the coordination of estimates, the decision of the President will be final.

2. The General Manager

The General Manager will be the representative of the President in all matters pertaining to the budgetary program and will have such authority in connection therewith as the President may see fit to delegate to him. In all matters so delegated, the decision of the General Manager will have the same authority as that of the President.

3. The Budget Committee

The General Manager, the Works Manager, and the Sales Manager will constitute a Budget Committee which will have supervision

Reprinted from James O. McKinsey, *Budgetary Control*, pp. 375–93. © Copyright 1922 by Ronald Press, New York, New York.

of the budgetary program. The Assistant to the General Manager will be secretary of this committee.

Under the authority and direction of the President, the Budget Committee is to consider all departmental estimates and to make such changes and revisions as it may think desirable. No estimate is to be effective until it has received the approval of the Budget Committee. The Committee will receive all estimates from the Assistant to the General Manager and will transmit the estimates as approved by it to him. In case the Budget Committee cannot agree with reference to any estimate, the question in dispute is to be submitted to the President and his decision will be final.

In the consideration of the departmental estimates, the Budget Committee may call on departmental heads to explain the reasons for the variations in their estimates from the estimates of past periods.

The Committee will receive through the Assistant to the General Manager periodic reports showing comparisons of the performance for the past period with the estimated performance of that period. On the basis of these reports, it may make revisions in the budgets for the remainder of the budget period, if it deems such revisions necessary.

4. The Assistant to the General Manager

Under the authority and direction of the General Manager, the Assistant to the General Manager will have general control and supervision over the preparation and execution of the budgetary program. His general duties are outlined in the several sections of this manual.

These duties may be summarized as follows:

(1) To receive from the departmental heads the periodic estimates as provided for in this manual.

(2) To prepare from these estimates (a) estimates of cash receipts, (b) estimate of cash disbursements, (c) estimated balance sheet, and (d) estimated statement of profit and loss.

(3) To transmit all the estimates to the Budget Committee with such recommendations as he may think necessary.

(4) To receive from the Budget Committee the estimates as approved and to transmit these to the departmental heads.

(5) To receive periodic reports prepared by the operating departments or the accounting department showing the departmental performance for the month.

(6) To transmit the periodic reports to the Budget Committee showing the comparison between the estimated performance and the actual performance for the period for each department, and to make such recommendations as he may deem necessary.

(7) To transmit to departmental heads any revisions in the original estimates which have been made by the Budget Committee.

(8) To recommend to the General Manager and to the Budget Committee such changes in the budgetary procedure as he may deem desirable.

He has the implied authority to do all things which are necessary to the proper performance of these duties.

5.   The Departmental Heads

The executive heads of the various departments are responsible for the preparation of the estimates of their departments at the time and in the manner prescribed in this manual. They are also responsible for the preparation of the reports called for in this manual. Any recommendations which any departmental executive desires to make with reference to changes in budgetary procedure will be transmitted in writing to the Assistant to the General Manager. It will be referred by him to the Budget Committee for consideration.

The responsibility for the preparation of the departmental estimate and the periodic report is in each case placed upon the head of the department. He may employ his assistants in their preparation at his direction, but the responsibility rests on the executive head in each case.

II. The Sales Budget

1.   Preparation of Sales Estimate

The Sales Manager will prepare for each budget period the estimate of the sales for that period. In the preparation of this estimate he will take into consideration:

(1)   The sales of past periods
(2)   The present market conditions
(3)   The contemplated plans and policies of the business for future periods.

2.   Form of Estimate

The estimate of sales will be made in such form as to show the anticipated sales to:

(1)   Hospitals
(2)   Merchants

It will also show the anticipated sales of each principal grade of goods sold. The first classification is necessary in order that the financial budget may be made, since the sales to hospitals are of different terms than the sales to merchants. The second classification is necessary in order that production may be planned so as to have on hand the proper quantity of the different grades. A form to be used in the submission of the sales estimate will be provided by the Assistant to the General Manager.

3.   When Submitted

The Sales Manager will transmit the sales estimate with his approval to the Assistant to the General Manager on or before the first day of the third week preceding the beginning of the budget period.

4.   Procedure by the Assistant to the General Manager

The Assistant to the General Manager will transmit a copy of the sales estimate to the Works Manager within two days after the receipt of the original estimate from the Sales Manager. He will transmit the original estimate, together with all the other estimates called for in this manual, to the Budget Committee on or before the first day of the first week preceding the beginning of the budget period.

5. Approval by the Budget Committee

The Budget Committee will make such revisions as it thinks necessary in the sales estimate, and will transmit the revised estimate with its approval to the Assistant to the General Manager within two days after it receives this estimate. In making its revisions the Budget Committee will make specific changes of particular amounts instead of making a percentage revision of the estimate as a whole.

6. Transmission to the Selling Department

The Assistant to the General Manager will transmit the revised estimate to the Sales Department immediately upon its receipt from the Budget Committee. This estimate as revised and approved by the Budget Committee will constitute the budget of the sales department for the next budget period. Copies of this estimate should be sent by the Sales Department to the Manager of each branch, indicating the quota of the branch based on this estimate.

7. Periodic Report from the Statistical Department

At the end of each period the statistical department will send to the Assistant to the General Manager a report showing the sales made during the period. This report will be forwarded on or before the fifth working day of the period following the period for which it is made.

8. Periodic Report to the Budget Committee

On or before the tenth day of each period, the Assistant to the General Manager will transmit to the Budget Committee a report showing a comparison of the estimated and actual sales for the past period. He will accompany this report with any recommendations which he may think desirable.

9. Revision of Sales Budget by Budget Committee

On or before the twelfth day of the period, the Budget Committee will consider the report received from the Assistant to the General Manager, and will make such changes as it deems desirable in the sales budget for the remainder of the budget period. These changes will be communicated to the sales department by the Assistant to the General Manager on or before the fifteenth day of the period.

III. The Production Budget

1. Estimate of Finished Goods

On or before the third day of the third week preceding the beginning of the budget period, the Works Manager will receive from the Assistant to the General Manager the estimate of sales prepared by the Sales Manager. Based on this estimate the Works Manager will prepare an estimate of the finished goods which must be produced in the next budget period to meet sales demands. In making this estimate the estimated inventory of finished goods on hand at the beginning of the period and the desired inventory of finished goods at the end of the period will be taken into consideration. The requirements of the sales departments for the period plus the estimated inventory at the end of the period, minus the estimated inventory at the beginning of the period, will equal the estimated production of finished goods for the period.

2.   Transmission to the Assistant to the General Manager

The Works Manager will transmit the estimate of production as prepared under the preceding section, to the Assistant to the General Manager within one week after the receipt of the sales estimate from the Assistant to the General Manager.

3.   Approval by the Budget Committee

The Assistant to the General Manager will transmit the estimate of production to the Budget Committee on or before the first day of the first week preceding the beginning of the budget period. He may accompany this estimate with such suggestions or recommendations as he may think desirable. The Budget Committee will make such changes as it may deem desirable in the estimate, and return it with the Committee's approval to the Assistant to the General Manager within two days after its receipt by the Committee. The Assistant to the General Manager will immediately transmit it to the Works Manager.

4.   Period Report from the Production Department

At the end of each period, the Works Manager will send to the Assistant to the General Manager a report showing the production for the period. This report will be forwarded on or before the fifth working day of the period following the period for which it is made.

5.   Periodic Report to the Budget Committee

On or before the tenth day of each period, the Assistant to the General Manager will transmit to the Budget Committee a report showing a comparison of the estimated with the actual production for the past period. He will accompany this report with any recommendations which he may think desirable.

6.   Revision of Production Budget by Budget Committee

On or before the twelfth day of the period, the Budget Committee will consider the report received from the Assistant to the General Manager and will make such changes as it deems desirable in the production budget for the remainder of the period. These changes will be communicated to the Works Manager by the Assistant to the General Manager.

IV. The Labor Budget 1. Estimate of Labor Cost

On or before the tenth day preceding the beginning of the budget period, the Works Manager will send to the Assistant to the General Manager an estimate of the cost of factory labor for each month of the next budget period. This estimate will be based on the estimate of production which is prepared by the production department in the manner indicated in Section III of this manual. The Works Manager will be assisted by the Employment Department in the preparation of this estimate. The estimate of labor cost will be made on a form provided by the Assistant to the General Manager. It will have the following columnar headings:

(1) Department
(2) Same period last year
(3) Average for last four budget periods preceding the one during which the budget is prepared
(4) Estimated cost for this period
(5) Distribution:
   (a) First period
   (b) Second period
   (c) Third period

Columns (2) and (3) will be filled in by the Assistant to the General Manager prior to sending the form to the Works Manager.

2. Approval by the Budget Committee

On or before the first day of the first week preceding the beginning of the budget period, the Assistant to the General Manager will transmit the estimate of labor costs as prepared by the Works Manager to the Budget Committee, with such recommendations as he may deem necessary. The Budget Committee will make such changes as it may deem expedient, and return the estimate with its approval to the Assistant to the General Manager within two days after its receipt by the Committee.

The Assistant to the General Manager will return the estimate of labor cost as approved by the Budget Committee, to the Works Manager immediately upon its receipt from the Committee.

3. Periodic Report on Labor Costs

On or before the eighth day of each period, the Works Manager will send to the Assistant to the General Manager a report showing the cost of factory labor for the preceding period. The Assistant to the General Manager will supply the form for the submission of this report.

On or before the tenth day of the period, the Assistant to the General Manager will transmit a report to the Budget Committee showing a comparison between the estimated labor costs for the past period and the actual costs as reported by the Works Manager. If the Budget Committee desires to make any recommendations to the Production Department with reference to labor cost during the remainder of the budget period, these recommendations will be communicated to the Works Manager through the Assistant to the General Manager on or before the twelfth day of the period.

V. Manufacturing Expense Budget

1. Estimate of Manufacturing Expense

On or before the tenth day preceding the beginning of the budget period, the Works Manager will send to the Assistant to the General Manager an estimate of manufacturing expense for each month of the next budget period. In preparing this estimate he will be assisted by the cost accounting department. This estimate will be based on the estimate of production which is prepared by the production department in the manner indicated in Section III of this manual. The estimate of manufacturing expense will be made on a form provided by the Assistant to the General Manager. It will have the following columnar headings:

(1) Department
(2) Same period last year
(3) Average for last four budget periods preceding the one during which the budget is prepared
(4) Estimated cost for this period
(5) Distribution
    (a) First period
    (b) Second period
    (c) Third period

Columns (2) and (3) will be filled in by the Assistant to the General Manager prior to sending the form to the Works Manager.

2. Approval by the Budget Committee

On or before the first day of the first week preceding the beginning of the budget period, the Assistant to the General Manger will transmit the estimate of manufacturing expense as prepared by the Works Manager to the Budget Committee, with such recommendations as he may deem necessary. The Budget Committee will make such changes as it may deem expedient and return the estimate with its approval to the Assistant to the General Manager within two days after its receipt by the Committee.

The Assistant to the General Manager will return the estimate of manufacturing expense as approved by the Budget Committee to the Works Manager immediately upon its receipt from the Committee.

3. Periodic Report on Manufacturing Expense

On or before the eighth day of each period, the Accounting Department will send to the Assistant to the General Manager a report showing the manufacturing expense for the preceding period. The Assistant to the General Manager will supply the form for the submission of this report.

On or before the tenth day of the period, the Assistant to the General Manager will transmit a report to the Budget Committee showing a comparison between the estimated manufacturing expenses for the past period and the actual costs as reported by the Accounting Department. If the Budget Committee desires to make any recommendations to the Production Department with reference to manufacturing expense during the remainder of the budget period, these recommendations will be communicated to the Works Manager through the Assistant to the General Manager on or before the twelfth day of the period.

VI. The Materials Budget

1. Estimate of Cost of Purchases

The Works Manager will prepare an estimate of the materials required for each budget period. This estimate will be based on the estimate of production prepared by the Works Manager as outlined in Section III of this manual. The Works Manager will transmit the estimate of materials required to the Assistant to the General Manager on or before the tenth day preceding the beginning of the budget period. The Assistant to the General Manager will transmit the estimate immediately to the General Purchasing Agent. On receipt of the estimate of raw materials requirements, the General Purchasing Agent will prepare an estimate of purchases to be made during the budget period. The General Purchasing Agent will make this estimate on the form supplied by the Assistant to the General Manager, which will contain the following columnar headings:

(1) Item
(2) First Period:
   (a) Estimated inventory at beginning of period
   (b) Estimated purchases
   (c) Estimated inventory at end of period
   (d) Estimated cash disbursements for purchases made during this period
   (e) Estimated cash disbursements for purchases made in previous periods
(3) Second Period:
   (a) Estimated inventory at beginning of period
   (b) Estimated purchases
   (c) Estimated inventory at end of period
   (d) Estimated cash disbursements for purchases made during this period
   (e) Estimated cash disbursements for purchases made during previous period
(4) Third Period:
   (a) Estimated inventory at beginning of period
   (b) Estimated purchases
   (c) Estimated inventory at end of period
   (d) Estimated cash disbursements for purchases made during this period
   (e) Estimated cash disbursements for purchases made in previous periods

The General Purchasing Agent will transmit this estimate to the Assistant to the General Manager on or before the last day of the second week preceding the beginning of the budget period.

2. Approval by the Budget Committee

The Assistant to the General Manager will at once transmit the estimate of purchases to the Budget Committee. The Budget Committee will make any changes it may deem necessary, and return the revised estimate with its approval to the Assistant to the General Manager within two days after its receipt by the Budget Committee. The Assistant to the General Manager will send the estimate of purchases as approved by the Budget Committee to the Purchasing Agent immediately upon its receipt from the Budget Committee.

3. Periodic Report on Purchases

At the end of each period, the Assistant to the General Manager will make a report to the Advisory Committee showing the actual purchases of the period compared with the estimated purchases and the actual inventory at the end of the period compared with the estimated inventory at the end of the period.

This report will be submitted to the Budget Comittee on or before the tenth day of the period. If the Budget Committee desires to make any changes in the purchases budget for the remainder of the budget period, it will communicate its directions to the General Purchasing Agent through the Assistant to the General Manager on or before the twelfth day of the period.

VII. Plant and Equipment Budget

1. Estimate of Plant and Equipment Cost

On or before the tenth day preceding the beginning of the budget period, the Works Manager will send to the Assistant to the General Manager an estimate of the expenditures for plant and equipment for each month in the next budget period. This estimate will be submitted on a form prepared by the Assistant to the General Manager.

2. Approval by Budget Committee

On or before the first day of the week preceding the beginning of the budget period, the Assistant to the General Manager will transmit the estimate of plant and equipment expenditures as prepared by the Works Manager to the Budget Committee, with such recommendations as he may deem necessary. The Budget Committee will make such changes as it may deem expedient, and return the estimate with its approval to the Assistant to the General Manager within two days after the receipt of the estimate by the Committee. The Assistant to the General Manager will immediately transmit the estimate as approved by the Budget Committee to the Works Manager.

3. Periodic Report on Plant and Equipment Expenditures

On or before the eighth day of each period, the Accounting Department will send to the Assistant to the General Manager a report showing the expenditures for plant and equipment during the past period. The Assistant to the General Manager will supply the form for this report.

On or before the tenth day of the period, the Assistant to the General Manager will transmit a report to the Budget Committee showing a comparison between estimated plant and equipment expenditures for the past period and the actual expenditures as reported by the Accounting Department. If the Budget Committee desires to make any recommendations to the Production Department with reference to plant and equipment expenditures during the remainder of the budget period, these recommendations will be communicated to the Works Manager through the Assistant to the General Manager on or before the fifteenth day of the period.

4. Estimate of Furniture and Fixtures Required by General Offices

On or before the fifteenth day preceding the beginning of the budget period, the head of each department will submit to the General Manager an estimate of expenditures for Furniture and Fixtures during the next budget period. The General Manager after consultation with the General Purchasing Agent will make such revisions as he deems necessary and transfer the estimate with his approval to the Assistant to the General Manager on or before the tenth day preceding the beginning of the budget period.

5. Approval by the Budget Committee

On or before the first day of the first week preceding the beginning of the budget period, the Assistant to the General Manager will transmit the estimate of furniture and fixtures as required by the general offices to the Budget Committee with such recommendations as he may deem necessary. The Budget Committee will make such changes as it may deem expedient and return the estimate with its approval to the Assistant to the General Manager within two days after its receipt by the Committee.

The Assistant to the General Manager will return the estimate of furniture and fixtures to the heads of the various departments immediately upon its receipt by him from the Budget Committee.

6. Periodic Report on Furniture and Fixtures

On or before the tenth day of the period, the Assistant to the General Manager will transmit a report to the Budget Committee showing a comparison between the estimated expenditures for furniture and fixtures for the general offices for the past period and the actual expenditures as submitted by the Accounting Department. If the Budget Committee desires to make any recommendations to the departmental heads with reference to furniture and fixture costs for the general offices for the remainder of the budget period, these recommendations will be communicated to the departmental heads through the Assistant to the General Manager.

VIII. The Expense Budgets

1. Control of Departmental Expense

In order to provide an effective control of the expenses of the various departments, as well as to provide the necessary data for the quarterly cash budget, the following procedure is prescribed for all departments and executive units of the business:

(1) Before the beginning of each budget period, an estimate will be prepared by the executive head of each department or unit showing the anticipated expenses of this department or unit for the next budget period, and sent to the Assistant to the General Manager.

(2) These estimates will be submitted by the Assistant to the General Manager to the Budget Committee and after being revised by it where deemed necessary, an appropriation will be made to meet the expenses called for by each estimate.

(3)   The amount of the appropriations, as determined by the Budget Committee, will be communicated to the executive responsible for the original estimate by the Assistant to the General Manager.

(4)   A monthly report will be made to the Budget Committee through the Assistant to the General Manager, showing the status of each of these appropriations.

(5)   The original appropriation will not be exceeded without permission of the Budget Committee.

2.   Classification of Departments and Units

For the purpose of expense control the various departments and units may be classified as follows:

A.   *Administration*
(1)   General Manager's Office
(2)   Credit Department
(3)   Purchasing Department
(4)   Accounting Department
(5)   Statistical Department
(6)   Stenographic Department
(7)   Personnel Department

B.   *Selling*
(1)   General Office
    (a)   Office of the Sales Manager
    (b)   Advertising and Sales Promotion
(2)   Direct Sales Units
    (a)   Each Sales Office

C.   *Production*
(1)   Office of the Works Manager
(2)   Subsidiary Production Departments

3.   Procedure for the Preparation of Expense Budgets

The procedure to be followed in the preparation and control of the expense budgets of the various departments and executive units given in the foregoing outline will be as follows:

GROUP A.   ADMINISTRATION

(1)   Preparation of Estimate

On or before the fifteenth day preceding the beginning of the budget period, the executive head of each of the departments listed under Group A will submit to the Assistant to the General Manager an estimate of the expenses of this department during the next budget period. The form to be used in the submission of the estimates will be provided by the Assistant to the General Manager and will contain the following columnar headings:

(1)   Department
(2)   Same period last year
(3)   Average for last four budget periods preceding the one during which the budget is prepared

(4) Estimated cost for this period
(5) Distribution:
    (a) First period
    (b) Second period
    (c) Third period

Columns (2) and (3) will be filled in by the Assistant to the General Manager prior to sending the form to the executive head of each department.

(2) Approval by the Budget Committee

On or before the first day of the first week preceding the beginning of the budget period, the Assistant to the General Manager will submit the estimate of the expenses of the departments listed in Group A as prepared by the executive heads of the departments, to the Budget Committee with such recommendations as he may deem necessary. The Budget Committee will make such changes as it may deem necessary, and return the estimate with its approval to the Assistant to the General Manager within two days after the receipt of the estimate by the Committee.

The Assistant to the General Manager will return immediately the estimates as approved by the Budget Committee to the executive heads of departments listed under Group A.

(3) Periodic Report

On or before the eighth day of each period the Accounting Department will send to the Assistant to the General Manager a report showing the expenses for the past period for each of the departments listed under Group A. The Assistant to the General Manager will supply the form for the submission of this report.

On or before the tenth day of the month, the Assistant to the General Manager will transmit a report to the Budget Committee showing the comparison between estimated expenses for each of the departments under Group A for the past period and the actual expenses as submitted by the accounting department. If the Budget Committee desires to make any recommendations to the executive heads of the departments with reference to their expenses during the remainder of the budget period, these recommendations will be communicated to the executive heads through the Assistant to the General Manager.

GROUP B. SALES

(1) Preparation of Estimates

On or before the tenth day preceding the beginning of the budget period, the Sales Manager will transmit to the Assistant to the General Manager an estimate of the expenses of his department including:

    (a) The expenses of himself and staff
    (b) The expenses of the direct selling units
    (c) The expenses of the advertising and sales promotion department

This estimate will be submitted on a form provided by the Assistant to the General Manager.

(2) Approval by the Budget Committee

On or before the first day of the first week preceding the beginning of the budget period, the Assistant to the General Manager will submit the estimate of the expenses of the departments listed under Group B as prepared by the Sales Manager, to the Budget Committee with such recommendations as he may deem necessary. The Budget Committee will make such changes as it may deem necessary and return the estimate with its approval to the Assistant to the General Manager within two days after the receipt of the estimate by the Committee.

The Assistant to the General Manager will return immediately the estimates as approved by the Budget Committee, to the Sales Manager.

(3)   Periodic Report
On or before the eighth day of each period the Accounting Department will send to the Assistant to the General Manager a report showing the expenses for the past period for each of the divisions of the department listed under Group B. The Assistant to the General Manager will supply the form for the submission of this report.

On or before the tenth day of the period the Assistant to the General Manager will transmit a report to the Budget Committee showing the comparison between estimated expenses for each of the departments under Group B for the past period and the actual expenses as submitted by the Accounting Department. If the Budget Committee desires to make any recommendations to the Sales Manager with reference to the expenses of his department during the remainder of the budget period, these recommendations will be communicated to the Sales Manager through the Assistant to the General Manager.

GROUP C.   PRODUCTION
(1)   Preparation of Estimate
On or before the tenth day preceding the beginning of the budget period, the Works Manager will submit to the Assistant to the General Manager an estimate of the expenses of his department. The expenses shown on this estimate will be exclusive of the expenses shown on the estimate of manufacturing expenses prepared as directed under Section V. This estimate will be submitted on a form provided by the Assistant to the General Manager.

(2)   Approval by the Budget Committee
On or before the first day of the week preceding the beginning of the budget period, the Assistant to the General Manager will submit the estimate of the expenses of the Production Department as prepared by the Works Manager, to the Budget Committee with such recommendations as he may deem necessary. The Budget Committee will make such changes as it may deem necessary and return the estimate with its approval to the Assistant to the General Manager within two days after the receipt of the estimate by the Committee.

The Assistant to the General Manager will return immediately the estimate as approved by the Budget Committee to the Works Manager.

(3)   Periodic Report
On or before the eighth day of each period, the Accounting Department will send to the Assistant to the General Manager a report showing the expenses for the past period of the Production Department. The Assistant to the General Manager will supply the form for the submission of this report.

On or before the tenth day of the month, the Assistant to the General Manager will transmit a report to the Budget Committee showing the comparison between estimated expense for the Production Department for the past period and the actual expenses as submitted by the Accounting Department. If the Budget Committee desires to make any recommendations to the Works Manager with reference to the expenses of his department during the remainder of the budget period, these recommendations will be communicated to the Works Manager through the Assistant to the General Manager.

IX. The Financial Budget

1. Preliminary Estimates of Cash Receipts and Cash Disbursements

The Assistant to the General Manager, working in conjunction with the Assistant Treasurer, will prepare a preliminary estimate of cash receipts and a preliminary estimate of cash disbursements for each budget period based on the following:

(1) The estimates submitted by the various departments.
(2) An estimate of the disbursements for taxes, insurance, and other items which are under the control of the Assistant Treasurer.
(3) Estimate of the collections from accounts receivable outstanding at the beginning of the period.
(4) Estimate of the disbursements on accounts payable outstanding at the beginning of the period.

The Assistant to the General Manager will transmit these preliminary estimates of cash receipts and cash disbursements to the Budget Committee on or before the first day of the first week preceding the beginning of the budget period. This will enable the Budget Committee to consider the financial requirements of the various estimates submitted to it.

2. Revision of Preliminary Estimates

After the departmental estimates have been approved by the Budget Committee, the Assistant to the General Manager will revise the preliminary estimates of cash receipts and cash disbursements giving effect to the revisions in the departmental estimate which were made by the Budget Committee. The revised estimates will be submitted to the Treasurer on or before the third day preceding the beginning of the budget period.

3. Periodic Reports

Periodic reports will be submitted to the Budget Committee showing a comparison between estimated receipts and actual receipts and estimated disbursements and actual disbursements. If the Budget Committee desires to revise other budgets because of the financial condition, these revisions will be submitted to the departments concerned by the Assistant to the General Manager. The revisions made in the financial budget will be communicated to the Treasurer.

X. Preliminary Estimated Financial Statements

1. Preliminary Estimates of Financial Condition and Results of Operation

The Assistant to the General Manager will prepare from the departmental budgets an estimated balance sheet showing the estimated financial condition at the end of each accounting period during the budget period. He will also prepare in the same manner an estimated statement of profit and loss showing the anticipated results of the operations for each period.

The Assistant to the General Manager will transmit these preliminary estimates to the Budget Committee on or before the first day of the first week preceding the beginning of the budget period. This will enable the Budget Committee to consider these at the same time that it is considering the departmental estimates.

2. Revision of Preliminary Estimates

After the departmental estimates have been approved by the Budget Committee, the Assistant to the General Manager will revise the preliminary estimated financial statements giving effect to the changes made by the committee in the departmental estimates.

3. Periodic Reports

Periodic reports will be submitted to the Budget Committee by the Assistant to the General Manager, showing a comparison between the actual and the estimated financial statements. These reports will be submitted at the same time as the other budgetary reports.

Index